Parents Forum

Where the Heart Listens

Third Edition

A handbook for parents and their allies
in a global society

by Eve Sullivan

Our efforts are dedicated to parents around
the world and to all those who care for children
and support parents.

Table of Contents

Disclaimer

Parents Forum is not a substitute for medical, psychiatric or psychological advice, for professional parenting education or for other counseling. Readers are urged to consult their health care advisors and other appropriate professionals about specific concerns and problems.

Licenses

We invite you to contact us about licensing the Parents Forum program. Parent group leaders, school administrators, elected officials and business and civic leaders, clinic and public health program staff, human resource managers, directors of public safety and correctional institutions, pastors of faith communities, as well as people working or volunteering in youth development, elder services and other groups and organizations concerned with family life issues find our award-winning program to be accessible, adaptable and affordable. We look forward to your inquiry.

Parents Forum, Publisher
Cambridge, Massachusetts USA
Contact: info@parentsforum.org

Distributed by Lightning Source
Third edition 2010

Support

Where the Heart Listens, first printed in 2001 with funding from Gravestar Foundation, was published online in 2007 with a grant from Reed Elsevier Cares. This edition is sponsored by the MIT Community Service Fund and Wainwright Bank. The Parents Forum website redesign in 2009 was funded by a grant from Tech Foundation and the site is hosted by Annkissam.

Heart of the Matter

Chapter One

This book aspires to change the way you feel about parenting, the way you think about it and the way you go about it. At the same time, it aspires to transform the ways we support each other as parents and the ways other individuals, agencies and businesses in our communities support us. Each task taken by itself is challenging, but there is powerful synergy among them and I am convinced that they can more easily be accomplished if we work on them at the same time.

Parenting is the oddest business: part service, as we nurture and guide our young people into adulthood, and part production, as we try to meet society's demands that our children become healthy, honest and caring, hard-working, fun-loving and service-minded young adults. Unfortunately, most of us are pushed -- and we push ourselves -- to meet these demands with ever-shrinking resources of time or money, or both.

In a sense, our children are our clients, consumers of our parenting services. Everybody else, that is, society at large, is a client, too, expecting us to provide a satisfactory product from our home industry. But where are the parenting schools? Who provides the on-the-job training? While these analogies hardly capture the many dimensions of parenting, raising children is still a job. We need to get down to business, starting with a careful consideration of the skills we need for the job.

This book is not fundamentally about raising children, but about raising parents. We need to become the best parents we can be, and this process requires that we reach inside ourselves and that we reach out to each other. Reaching inside ourselves involves thoughtfully examining both the parenting we received and the parenting we are doing. Reaching out to each other involves talking with other parents about our successes and struggles, and theirs. These two efforts, one inward and one outward, help us to develop skills to achieve our "personal best" as parents.

We must also continue (or begin!) to advocate for the time and support we need to succeed at this most challenging and critical job. Sometimes advocacy within the family is all that's needed -- help with homemaking from one's mate or children -- but we also need to advocate outside the family. Parents' voices need to be heard and parents' needs considered in schools, at the workplace and in government policy debate. The resources section gives you some pointers for finding information online about the many organizations engaged in supporting parents and in bringing family issues into public debate.

In developing new skills, will we become perfect parents? Of course not. On a good day, yes, certainly we will be good parents, maybe great ones! On a not-so-good day or a truly terrible day, we can share our frustration, anger, sadness or fear with another adult rather than take those powerful feelings out on our children. We need to reach out to other parents when we are caught in our own emotional storms and when our children's storms threaten to pull us in. In doing so, we can keep the best moments we have with our kids clearly in mind and heart. These best moments come when we are emotionally present in our own lives and emotionally available to our children. We need to remember how much we love our kids, how much our kids love us and how much they need us, even when -- or especially when -- an "emotional tornado" threatens. Other parents can help us do just that.

There are many books on baby care, child develop-ment, and children's learning, and countless vol-umes on the shelves by professionals and parents-who've-been-there about what can and does go wrong with kids and families. Still too scarce on the parenting book rack, though, is guidance for parents on specific techniques and strategies for dealing with the feelings and conflicts provoked by our own ordinary day-to-day experiences with our children. Most of us start on a positive path, with a lot of love and joy, and we want to stay on that path. But how?

A young woman who looks to me both as a friend and as "another mother" in her life (I am twenty-some years older) called me not too long ago to tell me that, after a year or more of effort, she had finally gotten a new job. She thanked me for encouraging her in the low moments. While her delight was obvious, she was emotionally "stuck" on one thing. Over and over, like a broken record she said, "I can't believe my boss (of the job she was leaving) didn't thank me." I listened, encouraged and then listened some more. My friend finally realized that it was better for her (never mind what her former boss thought) if she focused on the good wishes that other co-workers had expressed at her leaving and her own sense of

You won't find a set of rules in this book, no recommended bedtimes for a certain age child, methods for getting children to clean their rooms, or strategies to get teenagers to call you and tell you where they are. What you will find are suggestions for new ways to talk with your children and to talk with other parents about your own experiences. The suggestions will guide you in identifying your feelings and thoughts and in seeing how each affects the other and how both affect your behaviors. Often the feeling, thinking and action parts of our experiences get confused. The Parents Forum approach helps you examine your feelings and thoughts before choosing what to do or say. You will find particular emphasis on the practice of more attentive listening and less judgmental response.

I hope this handbook will help you develop greater appreciation for what is working well in your own family. Focus on the positive aspects of family life

accomplishment. Certainly it is important and freeing to pay attention to the positive elements in our relationships and our lives. Sometimes, though, telling a friend or a parent, a sibling or spouse, over and over again how sad or angry we feel, is essential to getting to a positive place. That conversation with my young friend reminded me that we never outgrow our need for a sympathetic ear and that if parenting is about any one thing it is about fostering our children's emotional development as they grow and adapt to changing circumstances.

will give you courage and energy to consider honestly the problems you face. The discussions and exercises described in later chapters will help you develop new perspectives on what may not be working so well. The handbook also suggests sorts of activities to look for -- and to organize -- in your community where you can meet others who share your concern for healthy family life.

But parents are busy people and you may already have enough commitments! Whether you use the Parents Forum approach informally, as a reference, or formally, through participation in events, I hope it will be helpful to you.

Most of us know instinctively what researchers tell us: that human beings, as social animals, need each other in at least two different ways: We need both the intimacy that comes from close relationships and the affiliation that comes from belonging to a group. Without these connections, we feel lonely and isolated. Participating in Parents Forum gives people a chance to make new friends and practice communications skills that can help us strengthen our relationships with family members. At the same time, Parents Forum activities connect participants to their communities, fulfilling the need for group affiliation.

You may have picked up this book because you are concerned about stress or unhappiness you have noticed in yourself or a friend or family member. Maybe someone gave you this book because he or she is concerned about you or your children. Perhaps you have young children -- or no children yet -- and you want to look down the road ahead to see what sharp turns and scenic overlooks await you on the parenting journey. However this book got to you, I am glad you have it in hand.

Perhaps you could say Parents Forum is a program of "smart love," in that we seek to create a better balance between discipline and affection in our family lives. In sharing our stories -- describing the events of our lives, our reactions and those of people around us, and the eventual outcomes -- we raise our social and emotional intelligence. We become more effective and more loving parents as, using the skills we acquire in Parents Forum, we learn to listen with our hearts.

Beginnings

Chapter Two

Parents Forum grew out of a serious family crisis. Some years ago, one of my teenage children started getting into trouble both in and out of school and began drinking and using other drugs. Within a year, his behavior was out of control. Despite the efforts of teachers, doctors, counselors and court officers who all tried to help us, his father and I did not find effective, long-term support for our son or ourselves in any traditional setting. My husband and I had separated not long before our son's problems began and we later divorced. In looking back, I don't believe that my son's misbehavior caused the divorce or that the divorce caused his misbehavior -- although certainly each made the other more difficult to handle. I do think, however, that the roots of both may be traced to difficulties we all had in communicating our feelings.

In our early search for help, the focus was always on my son but, in fact, I was as troubled as he was and didn't realize it. My fear and anger, my "control-o-mania," got in the way of everything! Successful resolution of our shared problems eventually came when we participated in a therapeutic community focused on recovery from addiction, particularly alcohol and other drug abuse. The program, which my ex-husband found for us through a friend, succeeded in helping us all make positive changes. I often wonder now whether improving our communications skills earlier would have helped us avoid many of the conflicts we experienced. At the very least, better communication skills would have helped us manage those conflicts more effectively and treat each other more respectfully. We found the help our family needed through Straight New England, a day-treatment program for young people with substance abuse problems. Founded in the mid-1980s, Straight was a controversial program

that has since disbanded. Its unique residential
component placed new clients in the homes of families of other young people who had been in the program several months or more. Parents received support for their own recovery (from "co-alcoholism" or
codependency) as well as training in how to guide
their own child and their "host son" or "host
daughter" on the path to recovery.

Professional addictions recovery staff directed the
daily treatment, interviewed parents and monitored
the "host homes" to assure compliance with state
safety regulations. Funded in part by families' medical insurance, through fees assessed to parents
and by fundraising undertaken by parents, the program had its critics -- and it certainly did not work
for everyone. But when it worked, as it did in our
case, it seemed to work miracles. The angry, self-
destructive teenager we brought to Straight became,
over the course of twenty months, a confident and
purposeful young man.

As clients in Straight for almost two years, our
troubled son, his brothers, his father and I, along
with several hundred other families, learned how
substance abuse affects both individuals and families. In Straight we learned that alcoholism, or any
addiction, is basically a disease of the feelings. With
a lot of hard work, my ex-husband and I each succeeded in rebuilding our relationship with our son.
This rebuilding was preceded by some "un-build-
ing," as we examined our past experiences to discover the interlocking, unhealthy roles we each played
under the influence of substance abuse. To accomplish this, we were charged with two main tasks.
First, we had to learn to be emotionally honest, that
is, to allow ourselves to experience our feelings and,
as appropriate, to express feelings, thoughts and

11

desires in words without blaming ourselves or others. Second, we had to learn to expect and encourage others to do the same.

Since that desperate time, now happily over, I have seen how putting the lessons of recovery to work in day-to-day family situations can dramatically alter one's perspective even if it does not always alter the outcome of the situation. I've found that the usefulness of these lessons extends to situations involving difficult people and challenges at work and elsewhere outside family life.

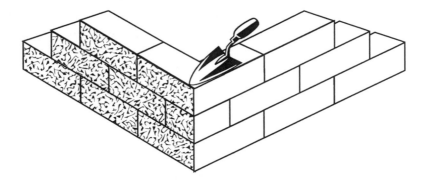

In the Straight parent network, none of us worried about the differences of race, religion, class or social standing that can loom large in ordinary life. We focused instead on the collective safety and individual recovery of our young people and, with those shared concerns foremost in our minds, we helped each other out. In their daily group meetings, our teenagers talked about past injuries they had suffered -- and injuries they had inflicted -- in their families, and they confronted each other about following the steps to recovery and the rules of the program. In twice weekly parent meetings, we adults did the same.

A central element in our parent meetings involved reevaluating a past incident we recalled -- for example, a night when a teen came home drunk, or didn't come home at all, or a time when the police called after stopping a young person for reckless driving -- and describing our feelings about the incident without accusing or shaming the young person. Limiting the discussion to one specific incident was essential, as it kept us from launching into a series of accusations ("And another thing...!") and kept both parent and young person "on the same page." Through this exercise, we parents helped each other learn to separate our feelings from our thoughts and to express both without labeling our teenagers. We also learned to separate our feelings about our kids -- love, admiration, hope -- from our feelings about their misbehaviors -- disappointment, disapproval, desperation.

Over time, we learned how to have honest and, at the same time, sensitive conversations about our differences, how to be both clear and respectful in discussing difficult issues. In my family, these conversations, at first awkward, were a refreshing change from the yelling, name-calling and swearing, and from the troubled, punishing silences that marked the time when my son was actively using alcohol and other drugs.

These conversations were different, too, from the negative view of family life too often portrayed in television situation comedies, where insult is humor and put-downs are frequently viewed as victories. In fact, to reduce this negative influence, television viewing for Straight families was restricted to a single approved video or a special broadcast on Sundays. Listening to the radio or to recorded music was also restricted, since the program's philosophy held that the messages contained in news shows and popular music undermined the recovery work that was our focus.

Straight clients and their families progressed through five phases before completing the program. First-phase clients, called "newcomers," were required to focus on themselves as individuals. In second phase, we focused on relationships with family and friends. In third phase the recovering young people went back to school or to work. In fourth phase they were given days off, taking responsibility for planning outings and activities free from alcohol and other drugs. Finally, in fifth phase, both young people and parents were given the privilege of standing at the side of group, in positions of authority, at our community meetings.

We drove seemingly endless miles to attend Monday and Friday night parent meetings and to take recovering young people to meet the van fer-  *rying them six days a week to the treatment center outside Boston. Sharing lukewarm potluck dinners, we gathered in the carpeted reception area of a large warehouse building, to socialize before the recovery-focused meetings. These always lasted too long, testing our commitment, I guess! In and out of meetings, we cried and laughed and sang. Day by day, helping each other, we got better.*

If a client in a higher phase ran from the program, the progression was interrupted. After returning or being brought back from "cop-outs," clients had to repeat the five-phase sequence starting with Phase One. This practice reinforced the importance of focusing on oneself and served a valuable purpose: holding teens and parents each accountable for their own individual recovery.

Long before I found myself involved in recovery with my family, when I began raising my boys years ago, I knew I wanted to be different from my own parents. But I didn't know how to make changes or even where to look for models. Although they loved me, my parents misused their strength and power. They doubtless had few models for effective conflict resolution and, as a result, their disagreements sometimes led to shouting, or worse, to breaking each others' possessions. Both the disagreements and the destruction terrified me. The fear I sometimes felt made me treasure all the more dearly the many happy times -- exploring the woods, raising chickens and goats, celebrating birthdays and doing ordinary art projects, crafts and gardening -- that formed the positive foundation of our family life. Unfortunately, while it may be true that the positive experiences took up more time in my childhood, it is my parents' rageful outbursts that occupy center stage in my childhood memories.

As a mother of young children, I repeated many of the creative activities that were so memorable for me as a child. At the same time, I found myself engaging in conflicts with my husband and my sons that were painfully similar to those I remembered from my own growing-up. While I struggled to provide adequate measures of love and positive discipline for my sons, minor conflicts, over dinnertime or baths, chores or television, easily became major ones.

When the boys were little, I could not see my part in these conflicts. In my son's recovery program, however, I learned how the tone of voice and choice of words in my response -- and whether I responded or not -- could help or hinder a peaceful resolution of conflict. As I learned to let go of the "control-o-mania" that was my addiction, I gave my son room to recover from his alcohol and other drug dependency. I became more solution-oriented as a parent and as a person.

Now that the crisis of my son's teenage years has passed, I can look back and see how other parents, both within the Straight community and beyond, helped me in my efforts to make positive changes and how, in our friendships, we refined our communications skills and created some new models for parenting. Day-to-day, my friends listen to me, sympathize with me, and encourage me. And so do my children, now. They also give me honest criticism, if I ask them.

A few years back, a co-worker related a story that gave me a painful flashback to my own now-distant crazy days. He had been riding the subway to work and saw a woman with a playful seven-year-old boy in tow, probably her son. She said to the boy, "I'm gonna slap you... and I'm going to enjoy it. Keep it up, wiseass. I don't find you amusing at all." My coworker was shocked and wrote the woman's words down to give me, knowing I worked with parents. What can you say when you hear a stranger say something like that? Could you say gently, "It's

Letting go of my need to manage things that are not mine to manage has been an uneven and difficult process with both intellectual and emotional elements. I may know in my head that one of my boys doesn't need help with a challenge he faces, but in my heart I want to do something for him. The reverse may also be true: I might be quite at ease not offering any assistance but have a nagging thought that I should say or do something to help, and I have to depend on my sons, who are now adults, to tell me if this is so. Since our children's needs change frequently throughout their early years and into adulthood as well, it can be a challenge to strike the right balance: to do enough, but not too much.

> rough getting out early like this. He'll be fine."
> Most of us, out of the hurt or fear or embarrassment that underlies anger, at one time or another use words we regret in speaking to our children. Don't you imagine that the woman on the subway was raised in a climate of verbal abuse and probably physical abuse as well? From other parents and in parent education programs, I have learned ways of handling my own emotional travel so that, for the most part, I can steer clear of such destructive confrontations as the one just described.

On a daily basis, I have to realize and accept that my children's lives are their own, separate and independent from mine. Ultimately, this perspective has improved my ability to listen to them.

I can usually hear what they have to say without recalling or re-experiencing the anger, fear and sadness that colored so much of the past. If strong feelings do come up for me in a conversation or an argument with one of my children, and I cannot resolve them then and there, I know enough to call a friend and ask for support, perspective and advice.

By talking with other parents and asking yourself hard questions about your motivations, you can see your family situation more clearly. Even if you find yourself veering off the happy and loving path you first envisioned for yourself and your family, you will be able to identify problems when they are still manageable. You may also be better able to seek

More than once, my youngest son said to me when I was on the verge of losing either my composure or my temper, "Mom, you need to call Bonny." Bonny is a long-time good friend who has A-number-one listening skills! My son had learned that if someone listens to his mother for a bit, she would be more able to listen to him. Perhaps a young person's endorsement is the best consumer report for the practice of parents listening to each other!

the advice and support of family and friends, or professional help if necessary, before a situation becomes critical.

I have seen myself and my children make small, consistent changes in the way we communicate with each other. They are adults, having turned 28, 36 and 38 the year this third edition is published, and two are married. I treasure growing friendships with my daughters-in-law.

My sons no longer need the kind of mothering I so enjoyed giving in the past. In a way, we are both farther apart and closer now. The space allows the intimacy first to happen and then to grow. I no longer pretend, or even aspire, to be a "supermom." Instead, I am content that we speak to each other often. We share worries, joys, plans and sometimes just listen to each other. On occasion, I need to apologize for something I've said or done and they do the same. What do you know... we're human!

Other parents have helped me and I trust that they will continue to do so as I take on a new role: grandmother. I hope this book helps you to ask for and get what you need from other parents. We can help each other.

From There to Here

Chapter Three

It became clear, about halfway through my son's treatment, that the habits of emotional honesty learned in recovery were helpful to me as a person and as a parent in many ways entirely unrelated to alcohol and other drug abuse. It also became clear to me that these lessons could be useful to people who did not have any experience of addictions in their families. Why not a positive program for parents who simply want to improve their family lives?

As a former teacher of English and French, I realized that much of what I had learned was, in a sense, a new language. If I could learn it, I could teach it. Further, I saw that the lessons of recovery could be incorporated into a program that parents

Aa Bb Cc Dd Ee

in any community could run for themselves. So I
started writing the lessons down. Then I started
a column in the neighborhood paper, *The North
Cambridge News*, in Cambridge, Massachusetts,
where I live.

Enlisting the help of friends and a college volunteer,
I began organizing activities. The first event was
a poster workshop for children held at a local
library. Entitled "What do you like about your family?" the workshop attracted a few individual parents
and kids, a group of children from an after-school
program with their teachers, and a reporter from a
local TV station. The energy we all felt that day --
and the media attention we received -- kept us moving forward. Next, we organized a book and toy
exchange, again at the library. Soon after these ini-
tial successes, we developed workshops and found
a school willing to host them. We did a "trial run" of
our format, which was based on eight fundamental
questions designed to evaluate our parenting skills
and deficits.

Many sympathetic community members and leaders, librarians especially, encouraged and helped us
in these efforts. In addition, I attended every parenting workshop and conference I could get to locally
as well as several in other cities and a few in other
countries. One good friend, another and then
another, agreed to help us incorporate and seek
non-profit status.

What should we call the program? "Positive-pro-
gram-for-ordinary-parents-with-garden-variety-kids-
and-day-to-day-run-of-the-mill-challenges" was
good, but too long for a banner. After a careful
search and much deliberation, we chose the name
Parents Forum. At the start, we proposed two

themes for our activities: parent support and family celebration. In our third year, we clarified our vision, mission, and goals, settling finally on three themes: networking, skill development and support. Some time after that, we chose the tag line "where the heart listens" to emphasize that listening, especially listening to expressions of emotion, is central to our program. That phrase became the title of this handbook and in 2008 we adopted the tagline "come share your strength."

While Parents Forum takes inspiration from the recovery movement, it also draws on my experiences as a "room parent" for over twelve years at my sons' grammar school, on 25-plus years of hosting international visitors in my home and on my teaching abroad: a year in Tunisia and a year in Portugal. In addition, my youngest son's interest in American Sign Language opened the doors for me to the Deaf community, whose members have a special bond defined by their gestural language. They also face special challenges in family communication, I realized, as nine out of ten Deaf children are born to hearing parents.

At an early Parents Forum meeting, a young mother decided the group was not right for her because no one else had a two-year-old. Certainly parents of older children could have given her some new perspectives on the misnamed "terrible twos" which can, in fact, be terrific! If my kids are boys, mostly grown, and yours are infant girls or pre-schoolers, does that mean we have nothing to say to one another on the topic of family life? Of course not! Exploring our differences and finding common ground benefits all of us, whether we are interacting parent-to-parent within a shared culture or across

In addition, I have been fortunate to have access to a variety of seminars offered at the university where I work. The advice and expertise of trained professionals on topics ranging from forming playgroups to financial planning has influenced me personally and has, in turn, influenced Parents Forum. In fact, perhaps surprisingly, some very useful perspectives on parenting have come from staff development courses I have attended at work.

While our children are not our employees nor are we, strictly speaking, our children's "bosses," our kids and our households definitely need managing. Management training can offer valuable insights on the dynamics of supervising and motivating others. What four-year-old doesn't need supervising? What eight-year-old doesn't need motivating? Even customer service manuals offer useful guidance. There will be times when the customer (your twelve-year-old?) cannot get the product or service he wants (movie money? a ride into town or to the mall?) and you, as "parenting service provider" have to say "No" clearly and effectively while retaining the

cultures. Besides the individual differences that may get in the way of our supporting each other -- age, gender, personality, education -- there are larger differences, such as race, religion, language, culture, and class. It does little good to ignore the differences. The best we can do is recognize and honor them. And try to look beyond.

"customer's" goodwill. All right, maybe that's stretching the metaphor, but I hope you see my point.

Still, as informative and helpful as professionally led seminars can be, they cannot replace the warm, personal support shared among parents -- for free! -- when we get together to talk. Parents Forum claims a section of middle ground between informal waiting-for-the-school-bell conversations among parents and informative (but sometimes intimidating) presentations by professionals on child development and parenting strategies. We certainly don't want to replace either one, but strive to incorporate good elements from both. In any case, we offer an opportunity for unhurried and non-judgmental parent-to-parent conversations.

When I meet someone new at work or in a social setting and the conversation turns to family life, as it often does, I am struck by two things: the depth of our shared concern for the well-being of our family members -- children, siblings, parents -- and the many differences that stand in the way of our sharing that concern.

Because our concerns, and our conversations, often focus on problems we face, it is easy to lose sight of the fact that kids are fun! Raising children is difficult, but it can also be the most joyful and rewarding part of our lives. It is surely the most important. When we are stuck in a bedtime battle with a four-year-old or tearing our hair out over a fourteen-year-old missing curfew, we may forget the joy of seeing our children take their first steps, of hearing them babble their first words (or seeing Deaf children's early sign-babble). But if we can keep the good times in mind, we have a better chance of

overcoming both the difficulties we face and the differences that divide us.

Difficult situations, from simple to nearly insur-
mountable, arise in every family, as do differences
of opinion. This basic, inescapable fact of family life
inspired a core element of Parents Forum: helping
parents focus on the way they handle conflict.
Regardless of our backgrounds, when and how we
approach and/or avoid conflict reveals our true values to our children. As they move out into the world
-- in playgroups, at neighborhood parks, in school
and eventually at work -- they take their cues from
us on conflict resolution.

As any parent knows, raising kids is much more
than a walk in the park or a day at the beach,
although these tranquil moments are absolutely
essential and keep us going in the less-than-peace-
ful times. For better or for worse, raising children

also involves the "screaming meemies" and the fall-
out from declarations such as "I will not wear those
shoes!" ... "I told you to be home on time for dinner!"
... "I'm quitting school!" and "I hate you!" These confrontations test our parental mettle. In Parents
Forum workshops, we help each other look at the
examples we are setting as we navigate and negotiate
our way through these day-to-day hassles.

Parenting styles can range from authoritarian to permissive, from dictator to doormat. Of course neither
extreme is effective in all situations or over the long
term. We incorporated into our program a model
(described in Mary Pipher's book *Reviving Ophelia*
and used in other parents programs too) for evaluat-
ing our parenting style that helped us find ways to
be authoritative without being dictatorial, and ways

*I have often found that a struggle (getting a child
to bed on time) or argument (getting help with
housework) gives me an admittedly unhealthy
satisfaction. Thoughts like "Poor me ...the kids
give me no peace. ...I do all the work. ...they are
ungrateful wretches" keep me from seeing the
good in my kid and myself and -- just as important -- keep me from changing the way I approach
a struggle. That unhealthy desire for self-satisfac-
tion comes, I think, when I want to be in control --
to impose my will on my child -- more than I want
to have a productive, if heated, conversation with
my child. The win-win approach to parenting can
work, but only when I give up the "kick" of control,
without giving up parental responsibility. Then I
am able to set clear standards and have my children follow the rules ....well, most of the time.*

to be loving without letting our kids walk all over us. At the heart of parenting, of course, in times of conflict or contentment, is communication.

As we developed Parents Forum workshops, we adapted tools from the Straight treatment program that had proven invaluable in helping my family resolve our communication problems. These include an examination of the balance in our lives (the handy guide), an exercise for identifying our feelings (feelings list) and a conversational formula for talking about feelings. With these, Straight had helped me to create a new base of emotional and intellectual honesty, right underneath my feet. On this firmer ground, I found the courage to ask myself questions I had not thought of before. As these evolved and the teacher in me wanted to share what I had learned, I wrote a simple curriculum based on eight questions to teach others what I had learned through such desperation.

One essential theme running through all eight questions, taking a purely personal view, is, "What is the role of this activity, challenge or conflict in my life?" The other essential theme, taking an interpersonal view, is "Do I need help -- or do you need my help -- with this?" As a mother I started out doing, or arranging or managing everything for my kids. I thought that was my job. But as a child grows, the job changes. If I hold on too tight or do too much, my son or daughter has too little opportunity to learn and grow. In fact, many of the struggles that come up in conversations and in our workshops have to do with judging when to hold on and when to let go. Simple role plays accompany several of the questions. These dramatic (and sometimes melodramatic) interludes help us look at our behaviors, especially on occasions of children's misbehavior.

From There to Here

With these roleplays and the discussions that follow them, we are able to uncover the issues motivating and the concerns fueling the conflicts we experience. In the process we often discover strategies for handling the conflicts in a positive way.

We believe that putting the Parents Forum workshop tools and questions to use in everyday interactions with family and friends can help parents discover -- or develop -- and follow the rules they need to be the best they can be, on any given day. Whether in private reflection, conversation with spouse, partner or friend, or in group discussion, the tools and questions enable individuals to clarify the issues that concern them, the challenges they face and the choices they have.

The idea for Parents Forum was clear: a positive program for parents. But how could we get parents who did not have any pressing problems to get together and talk about what was going right in their lives? We knew we needed to offer parents incentives or rewards of some sort, like the lollipops (now story books) that doctors give along with immunizations. So we came up with the idea of having a prize drawing at each of our workshops and other events.

In our early Parents Forum efforts to get donations of prizes (restaurant and book or toy store gift certificates, movie and museum passes) for parents, we found local merchants intrigued by our idea of a positive program and generally supportive. Some board members have joked that "No one has ever said 'no' to us" -- and it's almost true. Most people really want to support children and families in their communities and welcome opportunities to do so. These solicitations accomplish two goals besides meeting program costs: they get parents talking (sometimes even bragging) about how they are helping each other and becoming better parents and, at the same time, they let other people in the community know about and share in those efforts.

We had a small group of people committed to building Parents Forum as an organization and, supporting this core group, a network of friends and community people interested in helping the program succeed. Support from the business community along with recognition and donations from service clubs -- Rotary, Lions, Kiwanis -- and a few small grants have been key to our success.

From simple beginnings, Parents Forum has taken shape, somewhat different from the shape we anticipated. Our original goal of providing parent peer support remains unchanged but our approach to engaging parents has evolved.

Through early disappointments -- parents did not participate in our activities in droves, nor did they purchase our handbook by the dozens -- we realized, first, that agencies who convene parent groups are our primary clients and, second, that licensing our curriculum to these agencies is the most effective way to reach individual parents.

31

From There to Here

An unexpected partner has been a Massachusetts group, Children of Incarcerated Parents (COIP). An incarcerated father who had co-founded COIP posted a message to the Massachusetts Citizens for Children email list in 2003 asking for parenting education to be provided in prison. We began collaborating with COIP, collecting school supplies for children in their 'backpack project' and, with cooperation from the Massachusetts Department of Corrections program division, began giving our workshops at MCI-Norfolk. The experience of giving our workshops, about two each year from 2004 to 2008, has been, in a word, remarkable.

The first agency formally licensing our program was Parents Management Inc., Roxbury, Mass. (2006-2007) and the next was the Joint Committee for Children's Health Care in Everett (2007-2009). Both these community experiences have been very rewarding.

We continue to explore opportunities to partner with other agencies. We welcome inquiries from agencies interested in licensing our curriculum and, of course, from individuals who want to learn about what our program offers as well as from those who can share their talents with us.

Tools of the Trade

Chapter Four

Tools of the Trade

The tools of the Parents Forum program help us "tune up" our parenting skills. If you like the image of a car rolling smoothly along life's highway, think of the process as mechanical. If you envision your family singing in harmony, think of it as musical. Someone has to drive the car or direct the choir and it's us: parents. We have to be the responsible ones, even on days when we don't feel able to manage the household or mind the children and even when our children insist that they don't need us. We use our "tools of the trade" in exercises that focus, not on our kids, but on ourselves.

This chapter describes in detail the three basic tools we have devised: **handy guide, feelings list** and **conversational formula,** mentioned briefly in the previous chapter. Exercises accompany each tool and you can work through these alone or with another parent. Designed in part to help you consider your personal strengths and weaknesses, they will also help you identify behaviors -- both your own and those of family members -- that you would like to target for change.

With the first tool, a **handy guide,** you consider the balance or lack of balance -- and the sometimes competing demands -- of five areas of your life. These are (1) self-care and decision-making, (2) relationships with family and friends, (3) achievement in school or work, (4) leisure activities, and (5) community activities. To create this guide, put one hand down on a blank sheet of paper with your fingers spread apart. With a pencil in the other hand, trace your hand shape - just as you probably did as a kid. Then label your thumb, 1 - self-care, and the other fingers, in order, 2 - relationships, 3 - achievement, 4 - leisure, and 5 - community.

In a Parents Forum workshop we begin with this handy guide. Ordinary life rarely allows us time to focus on the balance among these five kinds of

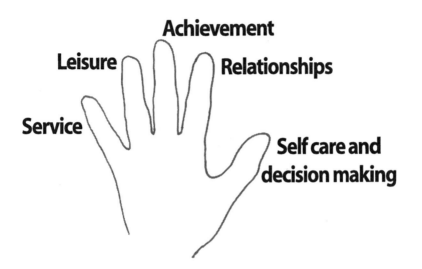

Achievement

Leisure

Relationships

Service

Self care and decision making

activities -- we are usually too busy engaged in one activity or another. To continue the exercise, take the guide you have drawn and note beside each finger something you have done in that category in the last week. You may find it difficult to decide which activity to put where, since an activity can fit into more than one category. For example, you can play soccer for exercise (self-care), as a way to enjoy the company of family or friends (relationships), as a paid coach or player (achievement), as something you do for fun (leisure) or as a volunteer coach in a youth league (service).

Taking another example, you may be paid to do housework if you work as a cook or cleaning person. Most of us who are raising children, though, do food shopping, cooking, cleaning and laundry without pay. Are these tasks less achievement, then, and more service? They are both, of course, and ought to be recognized as such within the family and in the community!

Almost anything you do -- gardening, cooking, carpentry, sewing, painting, fixing cars, caring for animals, cleaning, driving -- the practice of any skill or talent, can fulfill any one of the five areas. What you

As a new mother, at home with my first child, I sometimes felt terribly lonely, missing the companionship of students and other teachers. I felt jobless! I was working harder than ever but without the status of a place to work and a paycheck. I often wondered if I should get a uniform. Should there be homemaker badges, to be worn proudly by women and, now, also men who are stay-at-home parents? Recently I have seen designated parking spaces in some lots marked for "Parents with Young Children." Good idea! Official recognition could go a long way toward countering the ridiculous idea that parents at home with children do not work. We can begin by saying of people who are parenting full-time, "They do not work outside the home."

consider play may seem like work to me. My paid work may be the same as someone else's volunteer service. As you complete this exercise, noting an activity for each part of the handy guide, even if it is difficult to fit an activity in only one category, take a moment to reflect on the week gone by. How did you feel while you were involved in each activity? How do you feel now that it is done?

Consider whether the time you spent and the satisfaction you felt in doing each activity is what you

One workshop participant told a story of her five-year-old daughter coming home from kindergarten with a picture of the whole family, and there was mom, with five arms and hands. Puzzled, she asked her little girl, "Why does Mommy have all those hands?" The answer came back, "You're always so busy." She found a lesson there. Maybe, she realized, I don't need to spend so much energy and time doing things: maybe I need to spend a little more time just being with my kid.

would like it to be. Would you like to spend more time alone or on activities of your own choosing? ...with family members or friends? ...at work? ...having fun? ...in community activities? Remember that the exercise is only for assessment, not judgment. Set aside the "shoulds" and look at what you actually do. Consider what you would like to do more, or less of, without worrying about whether a change is possible. Limiting the evaluation to one week makes it easier to be honest and specific about the imbalances in our lives that the handy guide may reveal.

Setting aside the handy guide, we move on to our second tool, a **feelings list**. Creating this list can be harder than it seems, as our minds may wander off into what we think, or what we think we should feel, or how someone else told us we should, or shouldn't, feel. Take the handy guide you made and write a feeling next to each activity. For example, "I felt refreshed after my walk to the train station," "I felt annoyed about the expense of getting the car repaired," "I felt grateful for my health after visiting my sick relative in the hospital," "I felt resentful about putting in extra time on the school volunteer project."

Starting with the feelings that you listed for the activities you described, try filling a whole sheet with feeling words. Your list, if it's something like mine, may start off with happy, sad, afraid, angry (the basic four) and move on to confused (a convenient catchall if you can't come up with a specific feeling word) or perhaps frustrated, amused, relieved, lonely and so on. Often physical sensations -- tired, thirsty, sore -- are easier to name than feelings, but try to find words for emotions, as many as you can. It may be enough to make the list once and keep it somewhere convenient, in your wallet or handbag or on the refrigerator, but you can also add to it from time to time.

Making this list may seem like a tedious exercise, but it is actually very important. Because demands of daily life are often pressing -- our thoughts may come in a rush and events often require immediate action -- it can be enormously helpful to take the time and make a special effort to become aware of our emotions.

When our family started the Straight treatment program, we were given a feelings list. At the outset, I saw it only as words on a page and had no idea of the key role it would play in my own -- and my son's -- recovery. But my determination to do whatever it took to help him propelled me through the discomfort of examining my feelings. As instructed, I kept the list with me -- like vocabulary words in a new language -- looked at it frequently, adding notes and new words. I'd refer to it especially when I got angry or when someone got angry with me, as we were told that anger is often a mask for other feelings. I began to see the list's value in helping me get to the root of my emotional turmoil. When someone (a child, coworker or boss) interrupts me in the middle of a task, I may first feel angry at the person but then realize that I feel confused by the interruption. If I can tell the person that, or simply take a moment to catch my breath and "shift gears," I am able to respond more calmly.

Anger is a fact of life, sometimes justified and often helpful (for example, in warding off threats), but it is seldom simple. With the feelings list in hand, or at least in mind, I learned to respond rather than react

> *In more than one telephone conversation with my ex-husband, I felt angry enough (about money or custody or whatever) to slam the receiver down. He probably felt the same way. Keeping in mind the idea of anger-as-a-mask, I could see that behind my anger was resentment about losing time with my children -- his children, too, of course -- or fear about not having enough money to pay for the things or the activities I thought the boys should have. With that perspective on my own mixed feelings, I realized he had some of the same mixed feelings. This insight helped me to be less defensive and, usually, negotiate more reasonably with him.*

to my own feelings of anger and to angry outbursts
in other people, including my children. I shared the
list with many friends and, in developing Parents
Forum, realized that it had to be a key element in
our program.

Of course anger is not the only strong feeling. Fear
and grief can overwhelm us, as can more positive
feelings. People do, after all, sometimes weep for joy!
Somehow, probably from my parents, I got the
notion that being a grownup meant being in charge
of myself and "in control" of my feelings. This, in
fact, is only half true. While I need to learn to take
charge of my life -- think things through and act
responsibly -- my feelings are what they are. I now
realize that I spent a lot of my childhood (and my
adulthood!) resisting them.

Recovery compelled me to break down the internal
emotional dam I had built up. Dismantling that dam
involved two related tasks. First, I needed to let
myself experience my emotions, a physical process.
I did a good bit of crying -- and laughing -- in
Straight, as did just about everyone else, teens and
parents alike. Second, I needed to learn to acknowledge how I felt -- at times angry, fearful, resentful,
relieved -- recognize and name these feelings, a mental process. Ironically, in my efforts to be a good
mother, I had tried to teach my children to do this,
yet I seldom did so myself. We adults are generally
expected to "keep it together" but we lose something
important in the process. In learning to disguise our
feelings, often for valid social reasons, we lose contact with a wellspring of energy within us.

Whether we're laughing, crying, ranting or raving,
we can encourage and support each other. Our discussions in Parents Forum sometimes bring up

powerful feelings! Our love for our kids is so strong that it should be no surprise that the fear, sadness and anger we sometimes experience in dealing with them are equally strong.

Anger is natural, normal and important. It helps us set boundaries and right wrongs. But when anger takes the place of a full range of emotional expression -- as it too often can for men and boys -- either it becomes a shield for other natural, normal and important feelings or, worse, it can become a weapon.

I remember my father as a funny and affectionate man. When I was small he used to make up stories with me as the lead character and my teddy bear "Moanie" -- short for "Pandemonium" -- in a supporting role, along with the chickens that he and my mother raised in the backyard of the small town in Ohio where we lived. I remember waiting eagerly for the next episode of "Moanie and Chickie and Me." There were times, though, when the funny and caring dad I knew and loved "lost it" and his anger got the better of him. Those memories are equally strongly etched in my memory.

One of the scariest moments of my childhood occurred when I was about seven or eight years old and accidentally knocked a treasured piece of sculpture off a low table in our living room. One of a pair of ivory elephant bookends, it got chipped when it hit the floor. My father, furious that I had ruined something special to him -- even though I had not done it on purpose -- took the other, undamaged ivory elephant and smashed it to pieces on the floor. Although he

41

didn't hit me, I was terrified at his rage. I felt over-whelmed with regret that I had broken something beautiful and something he cared so much about. I must have felt worse that I brought him to such fury, but my overwhelming recollection is one of numbness and cold fear.

When I remember the incident I always imagine myself much younger than I was at the time, proba-bly because I felt so small. I certainly don't recall our talking about what happened nor do I remem-ber my father giving me a chance to apologize or make amends. All that remains is the image of him holding the ivory elephant up over his head. And me terrified, not even able to cry. With the benefit of hindsight -- and as a parent I "lost it" more than a few times with my own children -- I can see how my father could have handled the situation differently.

Perhaps, if my dad had been in a group like Parents Forum, he might have learned how damaging par-ents' uncontrolled expression of anger can be to a child. He might have known how threatening it is to destroy possessions violently. He might have real-ized the intensity of his anger and chosen a differ-ent way to express it. Perhaps he could even have cried. He might have given me a chance to cry and express my regret and my desire to make it up to him. Perhaps the piece I had broken off the bookend could have been glued back on. Certainly the dam-age to our relationship caused by such a rageful outburst would have been avoided.

Remembering the fear I experienced then, and feel-ing it again, yes, often shaking and crying as I retell the story, gives me energy to write this book. I hope my telling it will impress on parents how important it is for us to moderate our responses when our kids do what they do. Try thinking back to times when you have "lost it" with your kids and then further back to see if these experiences remind you of others in your own childhood. It is so common for us to inadvertently repeat our parents' mistakes despite our firm intention not to. When we recognize the roots of current struggles we are more likely to avoid injuring our kids in ways we may have been injured in the past.

Kids break things, come home late and mess up the house, but so do grownups. On more than one occasion I have recognized in my own heart a fury similar to my dad's when I broke that ivory elephant.

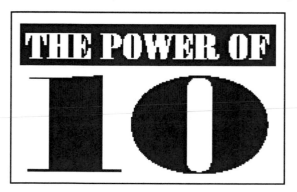

Now I work hard to remember to catch my breath and let myself shake or cry or perspire -- and count to ten -- then use words and choose them carefully, avoiding hateful, abusive or shaming language. As a less than perfect parent, I don't always succeed, but I have brought my average up considerably.

We are born having feelings -- a grabby one-year-old, a defiant two-year-old and rebellious teens remind us if we forget -- and we have to learn to be aware of our own and others' feelings. While a vital element of our job as parents is to teach our kids to monitor and manage their feelings, we are more effective at this task if we continually develop our own emotional awareness, if we "model the behavior."

43

Tools of the Trade

Until tuning in to feelings is something you do comfortably, it is really helpful to make time for this exercise with another adult, or with one of your children, on a regular basis, perhaps once a week, and even better, once a day. The end of the day, as part of bedtime routine, before reading a story, might be a moment to weave emotional themes into conversation with your children. Take turns, timed if you like, talking with your kids about how you feel. Individual reflection is helpful too. Mornings, if you get up before your children, or evenings after they are asleep, may be good times to do some journal writing on feelings. At the very least, keep adding to your feelings list. The goals of the exercises are to become more aware of what you are feeling and to become better at expressing how you feel, out loud, to someone else.

In our first Parents Forum workshops, we often found it difficult to get parents to focus on themselves. They would initially object to the exercises on the grounds that they should be talking about their children. After a while, though, by explicitly honoring listening and without insisting that people talk, we usually found participants entered into lively discussion of the past week's activities and their feelings about them. At the end of the workshops, when we asked for feedback, people almost always commented on how refreshing it was to take time to focus on their own feelings. One mother told us, "The workshop discussions held up a mirror for us to look at our family life rather than require us to talk about family issues. They were very helpful and challenging."

The handy guide and feelings list prepare the way for the third basic Parents Forum tool: a conversational formula. The first few times, or the first dozen

times, you use this formula, it will probably feel
strange because it is different from common ways
we express ourselves. In the midst of conflict, people
often say things like "You make me mad!" "Stop
bothering me!" "Shut (expletive deleted) up!"
The **conversational formula** requires that you
name the feeling you have, describe the specific
behavior prompting the feeling and then state a
thought (or idea, or principle) that explains the
situation. It goes like this:

I feel ___ (a word from your list) **about** ___ (an event
or behavior) **because** ___ (a principle, value or rule).

At first the formula can feel artificial, perhaps
because we so easily confuse feelings with thoughts,
or because we learned that some feelings are considered "bad" and are better not revealed. Practice
with the conversational formula is best done when
you are not under immediate stress, but the tool is
especially useful when feelings run high. A doctor
takes a patient's temperature and blood pressure at
routine check-ups in order to get baseline measure-
ments. So too, if we become aware of our emotions
in ordinary, calm times, we have a reference point
for times when we are stressed.

Here are some examples: "I feel frustrated about
missing my daily exercise because it is important for
my health." "I feel confident about my son's return
to school this fall because he has a good friend in
his homeroom who is doing well academically."
"I feel confused about visiting my homeplace
because a family member seems angry with me."

Of course, the same situation can generate more
than one feeling: "I feel relieved about my boss

45

coming back from travel because I'll be able to ask him questions about work" and "I feel anxious about his return because if I make mistakes he will see them right away."

It is easy to confuse thoughts with feelings. Sometimes the phrase "I feel that...," slips into our speech, usually followed by a thought, for example, "I feel that, to be fair, you should cook dinner tonight." If you give yourself a little more time, you might be able to say, "I feel resentful at having to make dinner again tonight because we agreed to share the cooking." Having said that, and even if your partner hasn't responded, you might be able to frame a request using a feeling word, "I would feel really grateful if you make dinner tonight." Notice ...no name-calling (You're a stinker!) ....no wild accusations (You never do anything in the kitchen!) ...no self-pity (When's the last time you even picked up a dirty dish: why do I have to do everything?). These histrionics do nothing to get dinner on the table or to enhance family relationships.

Also beware of using a word like "convinced" where a feeling word could go. You might think to yourself, "I feel convinced that my daughter is spending too much time with her boyfriend and not enough on her studies." Talking with your daughter directly, you might set aside your firm conviction (although you do know what's right) and say, "I feel worried about your spending a lot of time with your boyfriend because you are neglecting your school work." She might or might not share your concern for academic success, but you have been honest with your worry. She might realize that she's a little worried too, although she might not tell you right away.

Modify these examples to suit yourself: "I feel pleased about taking a long walk last Sunday because it was enjoyable and afterwards I slept well." "I feel relieved about having a telephone visit with my sister because we are each under a lot of stress and our conversation gave us both a nice lift." "I feel resentful about spending Saturday cleaning the garage because my wife/husband/kids didn't help." And, perhaps, "I feel accomplished about cleaning the garage by myself because it was a big job."

Would you ever be able to say, "I feel appreciated for cleaning the garage because my family thanked me, made dinner and did the dishes"? Doubtful. But realizing that you want both appreciation and help is a step toward asking for them.

Making a conscious effort to consider your own feelings is good for you in a number of ways. In the short term it may keep you from "flying off the handle" when you are angry. It can help you empathize with your children or spouse in their anger, sadness or fear. Taking a longer view, this effort to raise your emotional awareness can help you better organize your daily life. Look back at the handy guide you made. Remember that you were asked to consider what you would like to do more, or less of, without

worrying about whether a change is possible.
Now think about whether changes are possible and
what changes you would like to make. Remember
that "the journey of a thousand miles begins with
a single step" and be patient with yourself if the
changes you make seem small and the process
slow.

"Putting our cards on the table" -- describing feelings, behaviors and thoughts openly -- can help
us make the small decisions that lead to long-term
positive change. One person might recognize that
working long hours is putting his health in jeop-
ardy. Another might see that not working long
enough hours is putting his or her family's financial
well-being at risk. Someone else might, of necessity,
work long hours, neglecting to take some special
time with her child. Competing demands of work
and family often obscure our valid needs for personal time, leisure pursuits and community activities.
We all have the same 24 hours each day and need
regular check-ups, both on our emotional state in
the moment and on the overall balance in our lives.

Family life is under tremendous stress in contempo-
rary society and it is a serious challenge to find --
or make -- time for it. What can we do less of in
order to spend more time with each other? One suggestion is to turn the TV off at least one evening or
one full day a week. That is one thing anyone can
do to reclaim family time. But there are many things
in our lives over which we have no control: You or
a family member may become ill or recover from an
illness, lose a job or get a new one. Negative and
positive changes -- gains and losses -- can be
almost equally disruptive. External changes in our
family situation require us to change. Recalling the

handy guide, our first tool, you can see that as your family situation changes, you will need to reassess your time budget:

- When your children are very young, your time for community service is limited. As they get older, their activities can give you opportunities for service, like coaching a sport or leading a scout troop. Perhaps, however, something that also gives you time away from your family would refresh your spirit more.

- If you haven't contacted a dear uncle or sister in a while, maybe you need to take time to call or write him or her. Perhaps arranging for your children to visit grandparents would give everyone a much-needed change.

- It may have been too long since you took time to play, thinking mistakenly that it is less important than work. How about ten minutes for a quick catch or round of "hangman" (a spelling game) between dinner and homework time?

- Has your work become a bore or an overwhelming challenge? Is there a positive change you could consider in this area? What about regularly swapping some duties with a coworker? Many companies now organize their workforce into teams to do just this.

- This shouldn't be last, but have you been taking good care of yourself? You get to decide what it means to do this! A break could be 15 minutes for a crossword puzzle (my personal favorite). Small changes mean a great deal.

Tools of the Trade

Whether you are under stress or not -- and most parents are, some of the time -- it is helpful to spend a few minutes at least once or twice a week using these three tools to evaluate your feelings about what's going on in your life. In doing so you will see more clearly the problems you face and, with any luck, discover choices you didn't realize you had. Perhaps you need a walk, either alone or with the kids just for fun. Ask them to take you to the park! Turning the tables this way can offer a welcome, humorous break from the stress that comes with being the grownup. Of course, as a parent you will have to set guidelines for the role reversal. If your four-year-old is going to take a turn making dinner, the meal might be carrot sticks and peanut butter crackers, but nobody needs to go to bed hungry. And you don't have to cook.

Perhaps it's service that's lacking in your life. Doing a kindness for an elderly neighbor or for a younger parent would refresh your spirit. Only you can tell what you need and want in your life. And you can tell what you need and want only if you know how you feel. Keep the conversational formula in your mind, just the way you keep the thermometer on hand to take your child's temperature.

Unfortunately, the conversational formula does not guarantee results, either at home or in a public situation. If you tell someone who cuts ahead of you at the grocery checkout, "I feel disrespected by your cutting in line because I have been waiting my turn," they may say, "Well, too bad, I was here first!" or they may respond, "Oh, sorry, go ahead." You may -- or may not -- get the response you want. Whether you speak up or not, and whether the response is what you desire or not, the discipline of clarifying one's feelings is nevertheless useful. Recognizing how you feel can relieve your stress at the time, even if all you do is make a mental note to talk over an annoyance or anxiety later with a friend. In becoming familiar with the three tools described above, you are getting ready to use the eight questions that constitute our agenda. The power of the tools and these eight questions lies in the self-

Once it took me three days to muster the courage to do so, but I made an appointment with a supervisor and told her I was uncomfortable with the way she had spoken to me in a meeting. I didn't "tell her off." I didn't expect an apology and I didn't get one. I simply used the conversational formula, saying that I felt insulted, that I enjoyed the job and valued our working relationship. I can't say that it became perfect overnight, but it improved. There certainly were no more insults in meetings.

knowledge you acquire through using them, not in achieving control over your children. The example we set through our own behavior is a crucial component of our parenting. We must take time to carefully examine our expectations, motivations and actions. The questions help us do this.

Questions, Not Answers

Chapter Five

Questions, not Answers

Because people have been raising children forever, you might think the process should come naturally. But our instincts take us only so far. Parenting today involves everything from feeding and changing our newborn infant to helping our teenager with homework for a biology course only distantly related to the one we may have taken twenty, thirty or forty years ago. Our children, as young adults, may need more guidance -- on personal, educational, career or financial decisions -- than we can possibly provide. We need a range of skills that at times can be staggering, but we can feel less overwhelmed and can gain both inspiration and instruction if we share experiences with other parents.

Some child-rearing practices date from an era when children were considered property. Behaviors fostered by this power structure persist in families today, sometimes openly, sometimes subtly. While we no longer "own" our children, we are still the heads of our families. As such, we are rightly powerful. But with the immense power we have in our children's lives comes the obligation to consider how we use it. While we respect the many differences in parenting styles and practices, the Parents Forum approach is based on a fundamental concern that parenting serve children's best interests.

The eight questions of our agenda serve as starting points for individual reflection and for mutually supportive discussion among parents. Many of us find too few chances to talk with other parents and the rare opportunities we have are often rushed. There is simply no substitute for face-to-face conversation, as the spirited discussions that take place at school bus stops and among parents attending children's performances and games demonstrate!

We consider each of these eight questions in turn in Parents Forum workshops, but you can also tackle them outside the workshop format with a friend or family member. As we do this, it is helpful to remember that good parenting is a process, not a goal. We won't be able to give our kids every joy or help them avoid every anxiety that we've experienced -- we wouldn't want to. Our kids need us to be there emotionally for them, applauding when they succeed and sympathizing when they fail at the large and small tasks of growing up. At the same time, gradually and more or less gracefully, we need to let them become independent, even as we hold fast to the love and duty that keep families together. What to do? And when?

Experts offer conflicting advice. As a result, we may feel we are on a pendulum swinging between too permissive and too harsh, asking one day "Was I strict enough?" and the next day "Was I too strict?" Our goal in Parents Forum is to help each other strike a good balance between the two extremes, creating consistency while allowing flexibility in response to our children's changing needs. We approach that elusive happy medium in discipline in part by changing the way we communicate with our children.

At its core, this change involves replacing general questions like 'How are you doing?" with more specific ones like "What was the best thing that happened today? "What was the worst?" "Did you have fun in art class?" "How did that spelling test, soccer game or swim meet go?" When we ask about people and events our kids have already mentioned, they know that we have been listening and they realize that we are interested in them and in what's going on in their lives. By our example, we can help them become interested in other people and show them how to express that interest.

Questions, not Answers

This chapter will guide you through the eight questions as they are presented in a Parents Forum workshop and will illustrate ways that other parents have found them helpful. It is a good idea to consider all the questions on the easy days, when you are not under stress, so that you will be able to call up the relevant question on the inevitable rough days. Everyone has at least a few rough days! In the midst of a conflict with my children (and yes, I still have "push-pulls" with them even though they are living on their own), often ask myself what question might help resolve the conflict, or at least point toward a resolution. For example, is the problem about a concern (question two), or values (question four) or rules (question five)? Does the situation involve leaving or letting go (question seven) or change (question eight)? Specifically, does the situation call for a change on my part? Once

Upon returning to the paid workforce when my two older boys were in primary school, I sometimes arrived home after they did. The first words out of their mouths, as I drove up in the car or walked through the door, were usually, "Hi, Mom, what's for dinner?" It was an important milestone when one of the boys -- about ten years old at the time -- asked instead, "Hi, Mom, how was your day?" He hesitated only a second or two before continuing... "What's for dinner?" but still, it was a start! He asked about my day -- even if he didn't wait for the answer that first time -- and showed a new awareness: Mom is a person with friends, work, a life, outside the home. Now they ask informed questions, "How's your boss doing?" or "What's going on with your friend Bonny?" We should recognize our children as individuals and they can learn to return the favor. It's wonderful when they do.

you have worked through all eight questions, you can select the one most useful in a specific instance.

Workshops consider the questions in a number of meetings from eight separate sessions to a single session. There are two specific benefits to participating in a workshop. First, you take time away from your family and gain perspective simply from being away: a workshop serves as a mini-retreat. Second, you get the benefit of other people's perspectives on similar situations in their own lives and, if you ask for it, the benefit of their advice.

However, you can also consider the questions on your own or informally with your spouse or a small group of friends. Try to set aside some time, perhaps when your children have gone to bed or early in the morning before they wake up, to answer the questions, writing your answers down if you like. If possible, set aside some time with your spouse or a trusted friend to share your answers. You can also raise them in conversation with your children, other adults in your family or friends.

Your answers may be different from one day to another and your understanding will probably deepen as you spend more time on each question. You may find new insights each time you go through the series, so it can be useful to work through them more than once and save your responses to compare, over time.

An important element in the success of your conversations with others -- and a key to a successful workshop -- is a firm commitment to confidentiality. I will more easily share concerns with you if you assure me that you will not talk about them to

other people. A second concern regarding confidentiality is whether issues raised by one person in a discussion should, or should not, be raised by the other person at another time. Agreements about confidentiality should be clear. It is a good idea to mention one's concern for confidentiality at the start of a conversation and it doesn't hurt for people to remind each other at the end of the conversation as well. I might say, after telling a friend something that's troubling me, "Please don't mention this to anyone else and please wait for me to bring it up again." Or "Please don't mention this to anyone else, but it's okay to ask me about it -- I need the support."

There are situations, though, where safety is concerned and the listener should seriously consider breaking confidentiality. If a friend is talking about suicide or behaving in ways that threaten their own or another's safety, it is essential to seek help. In many localities 24-hour "hotlines" with staff and volunteers welcome calls from friends and family members concerned about someone close to them. Also, there are public and private agencies that offer mental health

Some years back one of my sons (a teenager at the time) confided to me that he felt as if life were no longer worth living. My first response was to discount his concern, but, feeling desperate and helpless, I forced myself just to sit with him. I asked him to tell me if he really meant what he said, what other thoughts he had, what plans he had considered or possibly made. Finally recognizing that he was serious, I knew I had to call for help. I called The Samaritans, a suicide prevention hotline, and spoke with the volunteer on the line. Then I handed the telephone to my son. He spoke with the volunteer for a few minutes and handed the phone back to me. The person on the other end of the line -- a lifeline, for sure -- urged me to take my son to the hospital and services. You may need support and advice yourself in order to advise or support a person close to you who is suffering acutely or who is at risk of endangering themselves or someone else.

In Massachusetts, where I live, certain professionals, teachers and others in human services, have the status of "mandated reporter." As such, they are obliged to report suspected incidents of abuse or neglect of children. As volunteers, Parents Forum participants and coordinators are not mandated reporters. The benefit of this non-professional status is that others may feel more open in speaking with us. Our responsibility as volunteers is to honor the trust people place in us. As appropriate, we urge participants to seek professional help if we see that their concerns are outside the normal range or if we see that the reassurance we offer appears inadequate to their level of distress.

If we were in a workshop now, the facilitator would say, "Let's get started," and would ask you to turn to the Parents Forum agenda. Here it is:

> *I did. That hospitalization was the first of several and the whole story is long and complicated. His depression had a slow onset and probably a number of causes. Several months before he had suffered the loss, to suicide, of a beloved teacher. Her death cannot be called the cause of his thoughts of suicide, but it certainly affected both of us deeply. The point of sharing this painful incident with you is to show how, in a moment when all I wanted was to turn away from distress, mine and his, I chose to face it and ask for help. I got help for myself so that I could get my son the help he so desperately needed. He's okay today, thanks to the volunteers and the professionals who helped him and helped me.*

Questions, not Answers

Getting Acquainted
1. What do you like about your family?
2. What concerns or troubles you about your family?
3. How do you express concern to a family member? How do you ask for and give advice and/or help in your family and community?

Getting Organized
4. What are your household values?
5. What are your household rules?

Getting Serious
6. What happens when someone joins your family?
7. What happens when someone leaves your family?

Stating Changes
8. What changes have you experienced recently? What changes do you expect in the future?

The following paragraphs describe how we present these questions in our workshops and share some of the responses participants have given. You may find some of the examples of family discord trivial or downright silly. This is precisely the point. If we consider minor concerns and our feelings about them, we develop skills for dealing with the major concerns and have a better chance of avoiding emotional blowups.

1. What do you like about your family?

In answering the first question under the topic Getting Acquainted, "What do you like about your family?" stay specific. Picture a happy time in the recent or distant past. Describe your feelings about the family gathering or event and about the people involved. Practice using the conversational formula, "I feel... (or I felt...) about...

because...." It can be more difficult than you realize to do this, as we may take happiness for granted. We do this exercise for its own sake and because recognition and affirmation of the positive elements in our relationships give us courage to face conflicts when they arise.

Time spent answering this question can help remedy that unfortunate family condition "Appreciation Deficit Disorder." If we remind ourselves to appreciate each other more -- more often and more openly -- we may find our family life improving and our satisfaction with our family life increasing. Saying specifically what we enjoy may be more challenging than "getting down and dirty" with what we dislike. When we give our kids and our spouses or partners informative praise, they know what to do more of. "Thanks for setting the table." "That sweater -- or shirt -- or haircut -- looks great!" "I noticed you made the bed and opened the shades -- the bedroom looks lovely." My two favorites in this category are, "Gee, Mom, you look great!" and "Lunch was delicious. May I help with the dishes?" although I confess that the second is not original to me.

Describing happy family moments and taking the time to express love and appreciation to family members provides a welcome antidote to the negativity we and our children sometimes too easily fall into. Children are more likely to express positive feelings if they hear their fathers and mothers and other important people in their lives doing so. Think back to a family picnic, or a day at the beach, when your kids had a great time and fell asleep in the car on the way home, giving you a full 45 minutes of adult conversation. Remember how peaceful and appreciative you felt. Reminisce about these pleasant moments, even when, or especially when, they are followed by less than happy landings as these same children, still sandy, but now awake and cranky, have to be given baths and put unwillingly to bed. Oh, those transitions. Remember to breathe.

Questions, not Answers

A couple involved in our program, asked how they were different from their own parents, responded that they frequently tell their kids they love them. The husband remarked that he often says, "I love you" to his son and, ruefully, described his own father's discomfort at hearing him say, "I love you, Dad." This couple said that while they happily do many of the same things their parents did, they realize that the parenting they got is not all the parenting they want to give, particularly when it comes to communication.

The shift from happy recollections to troublesome ones is natural enough, though. Most people benefit from a chance to complain. It's like letting off steam, a relief. In a Parents Forum workshop, we move to our second question, which gives us just that opportunity.

2. What concerns or troubles you about your family?

The second Getting Acquainted question, "What concerns or troubles you about your family?" faces the negativity head-on. Use the same formula, "I feel... about... because...." to describe a family issue that concerns you now. You can define family as the people you are presently living with, spouse, children or housemates, or you may define your family more broadly to include siblings, parents and children who may live elsewhere. You can pick a small annoyance (your ten-year-old or your spouse not hanging the bathmat on the edge of the tub after taking a shower) or a major worry (your mother's illness and diminishing capacity to care for herself).

For as long as you can, or as long as is useful to clarify your feelings, stay with the annoyance or worry without rushing to what might happen next or what you might do to remedy the situation. Our society is fast-paced and we tend to hurry. Emotions do not fare well under pressure. Just as we slow down for the good stuff in answering the first question, we slow down for the not-so-good as well as for the truly difficult stuff.

In a group discussion we move directly from this question to the next, but if you are working through these questions on your own, you might want to take the time to write down your concerns and your feelings about them. You may find it helpful to keep the list handy as you read the next section and consider what, if anything, to do about one or another of your concerns.

3. How do you express concern to a family member? How do you ask for and give advice and/or help in your family and community?

This last Getting Acquainted question is really three in one: "How do you express concern? How do you ask for and receive advice? How do you ask for and give help?" This set of questions offers a bridge between feeling concern (which comes up with question two) and expressing it. Notice the different elements within these questions: Under "expressing concern" the concern could be about oneself or about another family member, and could be expressed directly to the person or to someone else close to that person. Under "asking for advice and help" we look at our own willingness to receive, and under "giving advice and help" we look at our willingness to speak up to others and our ability to seek out and advocate for needed services.

In answering this three-in-one question, we consider the range of choices we have once we know what our concerns are. We may choose to do nothing. The concern may be none of our business and we may need only to talk with a friend who can be trusted to honor our confidence. We may wish to talk the concern over, in confidence, and then speak with the family member we are concerned about. We might offer some advice or help, or suggest seeking help from outside the family. It is important to recognize the continuum from concern to advice to help and -- just as important -- to pause before going from one to the next.

When I have a concern about one of my children or another family member, it can help to take some time before rushing to talk or advise or help. A situation may resolve itself. Or a night's rest and a new day may

give me a better idea of how to approach the situation. One friend has a 24-hour rule: if a conflict arises with someone outside the immediate family, she waits one day before acting -- or reacting!

In our workshops, we do a brief role-play -- and you can do this in your head or with another adult -- a "before and after" exchange of this nature. For the "before Parents Forum" version, you can exaggerate a worst case, an attack of the screaming meemies.

In my family, the Bathmat Issue is a classic, trivial yet persistent source of conflict. I found it annoying to have to straighten the bathroom up and put the bathmat back on the edge of the tub, after my teenage son had showered. He was quite capable of the task but I could not force him to do it. I'd start by telling him, honestly, that I felt annoyed. I might mention that I appreciated his helpfulness in setting the dinner table -- he's basically responsible -- and I'd ask him how he could remember to do that little chore. If I were feeling

Your kids didn't clean up their playroom and, yelling, you punish them with "No TV for a week!" The "after Parents Forum" version might be, "Susie, I feel disappointed about your not putting your blocks away because I reminded you about cleaning up before dinner."

Instead of an unrelated punishment, no television, you could impose a natural consequence, "We'll give these blocks a week's 'vacation' and get them out again when you can follow through on putting things away after playtime." This inspired solution to the messy playroom problem came out of a workshop discussion. The report from the parents who tried it is that it worked.

In the before-and-after roleplay; one participant volunteers to describe a difficult situation involving concern, advice or help that he or she faces. The participant may take an active role or may ask others to do so. With the volunteer facilitator as director, the participants act out the situation. Applause is allowed! The facilitator then asks for comments, first from the players involved, "How did that feel to you? Did you accomplish what you wanted?" then from observers, "Did that look successful? Would you have said or done something else in that situation?" The roleplay may be repeated, if time allows, with a different situation or a new cast.

patient, I might ask if he needed my help, that is, a reminder, next time. If I were feeling frustrated, I might tell him that if he forgot again, I'd impose some consequence, like an extra chore, perhaps cleaning the bathroom.

When my son moved back to live with his father, the problem was solved, at least in my house. In any case, he had learned that small household issues can mean a lot and that it's important to have clear rules and good communication about them, so they stay small.

Questions, not Answers

Still on the continuum of question three -- concern, advice and help -- we present a technique called book-ending. When a workshop participant needs to have a difficult conversation with someone, we suggest that they first talk with a sympathetic friend or another parent. They then go ahead and have the conversation or confrontation. Finally they review it, afterwards, with the sympathetic friend. Some examples of situations that might be made easier by such 'bookending' are given below. Note the progression from less serious to more serious intervention:

- talking with your child or the mother of your child's classmate about a missing (possibly stolen?) plaything

- asking a teacher for advice in helping your son discourage or counter his classmate's bullying or asking her to change your child's seating because of the bullying.

- asking a school administrator to change your child's class if the teacher is not successful in handling the situation involving bullying.

Any of these conversations can be difficult and the outcomes uncertain. I find such conversations less stressful if I prepare for them with a friend and can anticipate reviewing them with the same friend afterwards, in effect putting support "bookends" around them. In asking a friend, neighbor or coworker for support of this kind, it's important to be respectful. It's good to give the person the option of declining. They might not have time or might simply not want to be involved. You can say, "I'm having a problem with my child -- or sibling -- or spouse -- or boss. Could you give me your perspective on the situation?" Be sure to ask, "Is this a good time?" If the time isn't

right, but they want to listen, you can set another
time, and a limited time, to talk.

Afterwards, of course, say thank you. If you are the
person who listened, you can say thanks, as well, for
the trust your friend has placed in you. If you ask a
friend to help you rehearse a difficult conversation --
perhaps the example above, calling your child's classmate's mother about something the classmate might
have taken -- report back to that friend afterwards.
This second "bookend" gives you a chance to consider
how the conversation went and shows your friend
courtesy too -- he or she is probably curious about
the end of the story!

The ordinary complications of our lives, losing or
changing a job, moving to a new house and changing
schools, not to mention the extraordinary but too-fre-
quent complications of divorce, serious illness or
death, bring up intense feelings. Such events give us
opportunities, either welcome or unwelcome, to share
concern and ask for advice or help. If we begin learning to ask for and accept help early on, when our kids
are little, the process will get easier and over time we
will build a network of friends with whom we exchange

*A friend, the mother of young children, told me how
she talked to a neighbor about a problem she was
having with her husband. It was a personal problem, something she wouldn't share with just anyone. She termed it "serious, but not divorce-type
stuff" that had, nonetheless, left her exhausted and
desperate. The neighbor listened and then revealed
she had experienced the same thing. Surprised and
relieved at the outset, my friend went on to have a
very productive and profound discussion with her
neighbor, one that was very helpful to both of them.*

help. The primary benefit of this process is to us, as parents. Other people's ideas, time and energy can be of immense help. A secondary benefit is to our children as we are setting good examples for them.

We now move on to the next section of the agenda, two more questions on the nitty-gritty of household management.

Getting Organized
4. What are your household values?
5. What are your household rules?

As the workshop moves from Getting Acquainted to the next topic, Getting Organized, we present a diagram that shows four parenting styles. The volunteer facilitator presents this so-called "algebra lesson" before moving on to the questions in this section. The diagram helps us clarify the parenting styles

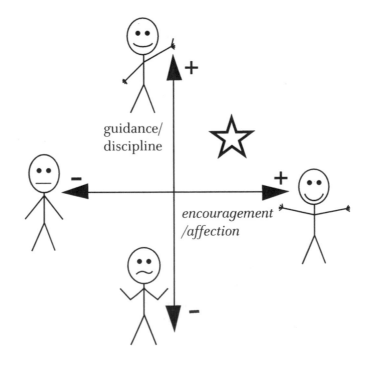

guidance/
discipline

encouragement
/affection

we use in communicating our values and rules to our children and helps us identify the effectiveness of different styles in different situations.

Different proportions of affection and discipline characterize these four parenting styles. Using the diagram as a reference, workshop participants are asked to share stories about people in their lives, during either childhood or adulthood, who characterize different aspects of these four styles. For example:

- your dad, who taught you subtraction when the nuns at school said you'd never learn

- your grandfather whose unconditional love helped you through the loss of a parent

- a demanding coach who went too far, insisting that you finish practice even though you were injured

- an inattentive teacher who let you slide by with less than your best effort.

Doing this exercise on your own is fine, but doing it with someone else can be especially beneficial, as each person's reminiscences encourage the other's. Think about adults whose affection and discipline made a difference in your early life and describe how they showed their care. Did adults in your family have defined roles, with one usually a "toughie" and the other a "softy"? Then think of times when you, as a parent, have been affectionate or demanding with your children. Ask yourself, or ask each other, what made you choose the "softer" or "tougher" approach.

Can you imagine having more flexibility in parenting, being, from time to time, more or less affectionate

and/or more or less demanding? Your children need
both affection and discipline, of course. The challenge
is to discern how much of each they need and when.
We get a better understanding of our choices if
we look again at the "algebra lesson" and consider an
important element in affection -- inquiry -- along with
an important element in discipline -- advocacy.

Affection does not exist in a vacuum. People cannot
have deep feelings for each other without knowing
each other and the process of getting acquainted
involves a lot of asking and telling: one person
expressing interest and listening to the other person's
answers. If we want to get and stay acquainted with
our children over time, or with any family member or
friend for that matter, we have to ask them questions.
That's how inquiry supports and enhances affection.

Discipline does not exist in a vacuum either. Parents
can get only so far with "Because I said so." We can be

*A defiant four-year-old challenged her mother, "I am
so mad I could pour this milk over your head!" Her
mother, completely out of patience, said, "That gives
me an idea," and proceeded to pour milk over the
girl's head. This memorably disrespectful moment
from my own childhood was retold many times for
humorous effect, but I recall it with sadness and
remember the retelling more clearly than the actual
confrontation. What was she thinking? Evidently
she wasn't thinking clearly. If my mother's failure of
self-control makes you wince, well, there are a few
incidents from my own parenting that make me do
the same, and perhaps one or two from yours as
well. My mother could have taken a minute to ask
me why I was angry and then responded. Her reac-
tion to my challenge was remarkable for its absence
of both inquiry and advocacy.*

more effective in offering or limiting choices and in setting consequences if we have well thought-out reasons
for our rules and if we explain both the reasons and the
rules clearly. That's how advocacy -- effectively communicating the rationale behind our actions -- supports
and enhances discipline. Like affection and discipline,
inquiry and advocacy complement each other and are
most effective in partnership with each other.

The importance of affection and the necessity of discipline are both obvious: our children need us to love
them and need us to guide them. The notions of inquiry
and advocacy may be a little more difficult to grasp.

The terms come from a workshop I took at MIT on
group process and were used to describe the two types
of behavior a participant may show in a discussion.
The advocacy stance, like the disciplinarian's, comes
with a raised voice, perhaps a raised or pointed finger.
In a parent's voice, advocacy can be, "You should do
this! Not that!" "This is right! That's wrong!" and most
important, "This is why." Discipline, in adequate doses
-- teaching and modeling appropriate behavior -- is
essential to good parenting, of course. Effective parents
stand for something, but we need to temper our advocacy with inquiry. "What is going on?" "Do you think
that is a good idea?" "How can you settle that disagree-
ment?" "Do you need my help right now?" A parent
using advocacy in the extreme becomes a dictator and
a parent using inquiry in the extreme turns into a
doormat. We've all seen parents who give a young child
too many choices. Figuring out how much to ask and
how much to tell is not easy, even if one has settled the
twin issues of what to ask and what to tell.

Further complicating a parent's job is the fact that the
balance between advocacy and inquiry is bound to
change as a young person moves through childhood

Questions, not Answers

into adolescence, shifting more toward inquiry. "What happened? How did you feel? When did you decide to do that (for example, to misbehave)? Who was with you? Would you do the same thing again?" Advocacy has a kind of built-in reinforcement for a parent -- "I'm doing my job; I am the adult here!" -- and can be

I recently came across notes I had written on a New Year's Eve, over ten years ago now, about a distressing incident involving one of my sons. He was living at his dad's house and was supposed to be out with friends. He certainly did not have permission to have company at my house. When I arrived home at 10:30, after ushering at a concert, I found him there with two girls, both his classmates, and one guy who was the older brother of one of the girls.

The stage was set for either a big lecture on choices and consequences regarding alcohol and other drugs, or screaming and yelling about rules and punishments: "This is a sober home. Drinking at your age is both dangerous and illegal." But, surprising myself, I chose a response with some advocacy, certainly, but more weighted toward inquiry, either out of shock or sadness. I managed to keep a low tone of voice and I hope I may even have sounded gracious to my son's friends, one of whom I had never met. "This is not acceptable. You need to leave now. I am very disappointed. It's cold. I'll drive you home. Please clean the counter now. Tomorrow you will come back and clean the floor."

I was furious, but I didn't yell. I clearly expressed my disapproval, disappointment and concern. According to my notes -- and the fact that I wrote notes at all reveals the progress I'd made in becoming more thoughtful and deliberate as a parent-- I called my ex-husband and the mother of one of the girls.

over-used, despite the fact that, ultimately, inquiry may be more effective. If I say something in a convincing and assertive tone, the sound of my words tells me I'm right, even if what I say doesn't convince my child. Inquiry, on the other hand, can be frustrating for a parent, as it opens the door to challenge or at least

My son and one of the girls were quite clearly intoxicated or high and I repeatedly urged them to let me drive them home. They refused but assured me that they would go directly home, a walk of only a few blocks. I let them go. Was that the right thing to do? I'm not sure. I remember feeling angry and helpless at the same time but relieved to be able to contact the other parents concerned. Looking back I'm not sure if this episode should go in the 'loss' or the 'win' column. Maybe it was a tie: a loss in that it happened at all and a win in that I handled it calmly.

I guess the reason I wrote things down was to be able to be clear about what happened when I talked to my son the next day about his blatant disrespect for my house rules and about his lack of concern for his and his friends' health and safety.

Probably I could have done more inquiry at the time. I certainly did the next day, when I again called my ex-husband and the parents of the other young people. That night it seemed as if I wouldn't get sensible answers to the questions I wanted to ask, "Who got the alcohol? Where did the marijuana come from?" so I let them go, both the questions and the young people. How different that exchange was from earlier years when another son acted out in similar ways, and we lashed out at each other verbally. I still regret those "first drafts" at parenting.

a different view. Asking my son a question about his behavior (or misbehavior) may be more difficult than telling him right off the bat what I think and what I think he should do. Doing so, however, may lead him to share information or feelings that could help me respond more effectively.

The choice between advocacy and inquiry can be a tough call. As the chapter title promised, Parents Forum gives you questions, not answers, and suggests ways you can evaluate your parenting on an ongoing basis. If you catch yourself "advocating up a storm," yelling or arguing forcefully to shut off challenge from your child, it's good to notice what you are doing and consider whether it is working. If you take the other tack and try a strong dose of inquiry, the same holds true. Ask yourself if what you did worked for you and for your kid, in that situation. Ask your young person the same thing, not giving them the authority to decide how you should behave as a parent, but asking them, perhaps, "Was what I did or what I said helpful to you?

A key to determining whether a child needs more dis- cipline or affection, more advocacy or inquiry, is his or her developmental stage. People who study on-the-job training for adults have identified four stages involved in learning any new task. Margaret Ann Gray, a staff development specialist at MIT where I work, character- ized these stages by giving them animal names: puppy, snail, donkey and eagle. In a workshop on how to manage volunteers effectively, she described a new vol- unteer as a puppy, a somewhat experienced volunteer as a snail, a more experienced but not yet fully compe- tent volunteer as a donkey and the 'ace' volunteer as an eagle.

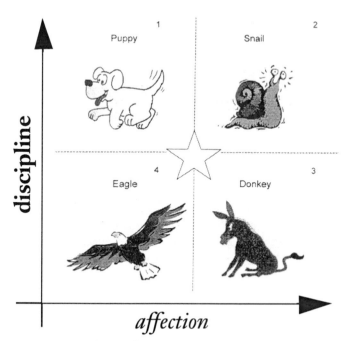

I was struck by the aptness of these images to young people's development. A little kid has many of the attitudes and behaviors -- as well as the appeal -- of a puppy. A school-age child, like a snail, seems to take forever doing the simplest things. I recall a dad at my sons' school once saying his fourth-grade daughter took so long to complete a task that waiting for her to finish was "like watching paint dry." Then there is the teenager, stubborn as a donkey, who really needs more carrot and less stick, more encouragement and less direction. Why didn't anyone tell me this before?! It would have spared my teenagers and me considerable grief. The eagle image is clear, too, of course. We want our young adult children to take wing and fly on their own.

Yet even our grown children sometimes need our direction and encouragement and we want to give both when we can. I certainly look forward to having my sons visit their childhood 'nest' from time to time, even after they've rented, bought or built their own. Parents in many cultures expect young adults to live in the family home for extended periods. When one of my sons moved back home for a few weeks, we had to talk through our understanding so that the arrangement felt like moving forward, not back, to both of us.

In Parents Forum workshops, participants are asked how they have balanced discipline with affection at their children's different stages of development by sharing anecdotes that illustrate their own parenting strategies, both successful and unsuccessful. Discussions can get quite animated, as parents describe progress through their own developmental stages. A common adage says that good judgment comes from experience and experience comes from bad judgment. We can learn from each other and perhaps avoid some of the more serious misjudgments and mistakes.

It's all well and good to understand that a toddler learning to use the toilet or to put on his jacket will go through these four stages. It is helpful to know that the six-or seven-year old learning to set the table, ride a bike or do addition, will also go through these stages. We can even see the adolescent venturing into the world of dating and the world of work behaving, in turn, like a puppy, snail, donkey and eagle. What may be less apparent -- yet equally important -- is the fact that we, as parents, go through similar stages. To many of us, parenting seemed relatively easy and fun at the beginning, even if the hours were long. As the kids got a little older, the job got harder and seemed endless. Finally, when I had worked through my insecurities and resentments, the donkey stage, and was beginning to feel confident and ready to soar, OH NO, my child had progressed to a new stage and needed me to start all over, it seemed, to develop a different parenting style.

It may be helpful to set aside some time to reflect on your own experiences with discipline and affection in your childhood, as well as in your adult work life and your parenting. Think, for example, of a time when someone was especially clear and encouraging in explaining something to you. Think of a time when the encouragement you wanted was not forthcoming from a parent, teacher, or boss. Think of a time when you "hit the right note" with a child in your life. You knew you gave him or her exactly the right "dose" of whatever he or she needed. It is just as important to remember the positive experiences as it is to be honest about the negative ones. In workshops, participants share both successes and struggles.

Workshop facilitators are asked to thank each person for whatever they say, without repeating, rephrasing or commenting on what the person said. If someone asks for feedback, of course, it can be given, but it is not imposed. Quiet participants are thanked also, since listening is as essential to our workshops as talking.

At this point, in a workshop, we acknowledge the work participants have done so far in going through these questions. Why not take a break before going on to the next section of our agenda? We do break here in our workshops.

4. What are your household values?

In Getting Organized, we consider two questions separately. You might find it difficult to answer question four, on values, without linking these to rules, but we make a distinction, as values presumably stay constant while rules need to change as your children grow. If we were talking together, doubtless we would come up with some basic, universal values: respect, honesty, cleanliness and good citizenship.

Questions, not Answers

In workshops, a volunteer facilitator asks participants to write several values they consider important on a small card and collects the cards. The facilitator reads several or all of the cards (without indicating who wrote what) and asks people to comment, if they wish, describing how the value is demonstrated in their family. For example, "good nutrition" might elicit the comment, "I usually serve water, milk or juice to my kids instead of soda." "Honesty" ... "My kid returned a wallet to its owner." "Kindness" ... "My neighbor puts my trash bins in for me on trash day." "Responsibility" ... "I encourage my children to take good care of their pet."

The exercise of writing down values is a good one for a couple or a family to do together. The exercise may reveal conflicting values that underlie conflicts we experience when we interact with other people. It may also help clarify conflicts that arise between important values.

A classic conflict is between kindness and honesty. Do you tell a family member or friend that he's gained or lost a lot of weight? It may be true that he has, but you may feel uncomfortable, thinking it unkind, to tell him so. Yet your friendship may be one that can accommodate or that even demands such honesty. These issues are ones that you may not have thought about or discussed. You may find that family members disagree, but the discussion can give you insight into the conflicts you experience.

What about conflicts between play and work, both important? What if I want to watch television (the value of enjoyment) and you think I should be folding laundry (the values of keeping the house in good order and being nicely dressed for school or work)? Maybe that's too easy. Of course you can fold laundry while watching television. But can your child do homework and watch television at the same time? Conflicts can arise over countless issues, large and small. So we clarify the values, as well as the feelings, behind our behaviors in order to more carefully and effectively "pick our battles."

Two more values that may conflict are neatness and creativity. If both are important to you, you might consider when and how these clash and then re-write your household rules accordingly. A sewing, painting, cooking or carpentry project might completely take over one room in the house or apartment. Who did the project? Who gets annoyed? Who cleans up? If you like to do creative projects yourself and want to promote creativity in your children, you might decide to "surrender and not scream at the messes," as one mother said. You could set boundaries on the creativity, that is, the messiness, in space and/or time, confining projects to a playroom table to be straightened up at least once a week. If we take some time to get clear in our own minds about what's important and what's realistic, we are much more likely to establish effective rules and to get our kids to follow them.

5. What are your household rules?

After values, we consider rules. This can be difficult. Two parents may agree on values but disagree on rules, as can parents and grandparents. But even if you disagree on values, you may find you can agree on some basic rules, if for different reasons. Often, we realize that we have never really examined or clarified the issues of values or rules for ourselves individually, as a couple or as a family.

If your family or household members are willing, after writing a list of the values you share, you can start trying to figure out what the actual rules are. Does mom or dad do all the cooking (yard work, animal

care, driving or car repair) or are jobs shared? Who
does the food shopping? Is it dad or mom who reads
bedtime stories or do they take turns? Who washes
the bathtub and who balances the checkbook? Who
buys and wraps birthday and holiday presents? Who
decides how much money to spend on necessities,
entertainment, gifts, vacation trips and holiday cele-
brations? Who shops for what? Who cleans what?
What responsibilities do children have at what ages?

Probably more important than any individual rule are
these considerations: Who decides who does what?
How are rules made in your household? How are they
changed? How do people know if the rules have
changed? While these questions are fundamental,
they are seldom discussed. We tend to deal with
issues as they come up, day to day.

If I believe adequate sleep to be important, what time
do I tell my teenager be home on weeknights? Parents
need to be clear on their absolute values and at the
same time be ready, from time to time, to negotiate
changes in the rules. As just mentioned, we need to
give some thought to when and how the rules get
suspended or permanently changed. For example,
a 13-year-old wants to sleep over at a friend's house
on a weeknight and the rule is that sleepovers are
allowed only on weekends. The parent might allow
a suspension of the rule if the child asks in advance
and there is a special reason, perhaps a school outing
the next day.

Of course, mom or dad may have different answers,
so parents have to communicate with each other, as
best they can, whether they are living together
or not. Children often develop a keen sense of who
decides what in a family, even when parents don't
explicitly defer to one another. And when parents do

this, responding "Ask your mother" or "Ask your father" to a child's request, it can be helpful for the parents to have a follow-up discussion. Even if your spouse or partner is unwilling to devote time to talking over these questions on values and rules, the process is valuable for the parent who does it. He or she can be clearer in his or her own mind about such issues as these:

- Am I being consistent for the sake of consistency or my own convenience or am I perhaps abusing my authority -- "on a power trip"?

- Should I involve or not involve my child in negotiating an exception to a rule?

- If I make an exception will my child take it as a change in the rule?

- If I do change a rule, should the change be made on a trial basis for a specified period of time?

- If I uphold a rule and my child breaks it, do I impose reasonable consequences?

The conversational formula can be used anywhere in the discussion to help family members understand each other's points of view. The 13-year-old might say, "I feel frustrated about your not letting me sleep over at Janie's house because Rebecca's mother is letting her sleep over" (a refined version of "All the kids are doing it"). Mom might respond, "I feel anxious about your wanting to sleep over because you won't get enough rest to do well in school the next day or to enjoy the outing" and might hold the line with a brief, "No, you can't go." There might be a more serious reason to say no. Perhaps the mother is not confident

81

that parental supervision at the other home will be adequate. A call to the other home, in that case, might reassure her or might confirm her decision to say no. On the other hand, the mother might express the same feeling but follow up with, "If you come home and take a nap the afternoon before, I will make an exception to the rule." The pattern we set for our own decision-making is one that our children often imitate, perhaps only when they are done rebelling against it.

It can be helpful to write a values and rules statement for your family. If you like, go back to the handy guide and write down a few values for each element of your life: self, relationships, achievement, leisure and service. Start with a few words on each element and describe the values or principles you hold and the rules or practices that follow from them. Include some principles you follow in caring for your home and possessions. It won't be etched in stone, of course. One page on the refrigerator is good enough.

Even if your family "mission statement" is very simple, it can be a helpful guide. If someone starts yelling, the person being yelled at can point out that a household value is kindness and that he, the "yellee," feels hurt or scared by the "yeller's" tone of voice. Just a suggestion. Remember this book did not promise answers, only questions.

As you think of the rules you make for your children, it may be helpful to think about the responsibilities you face as a parent. Your basic responsibility is to support your family. First and foremost you need to make sure, to the best of your ability, to provide food, clothing, shelter, access to medical care and access to educational opportunity for your children. Raising a child takes about twenty years and over those years, your job is re-defined each time your child learns to do something for himself. A newborn requires total care. A ten-year-old has doubtless learned to take responsibility for most basic necessities. A twenty-year-old may be living at home as a young adult or may be independent. The progression involves continual self-examination and re-evaluation of household rules. Family members may never be in complete agreement, but for a household to hold together, they have to reach some consensus.

We move on now to the next section of the agenda. In workshops, this is the halfway point and you can take it as a good time for a break. Put the book down. Breathe. Take a nap or a walk, if you can. Have a snack. Perhaps do some simple physical chore -- mow the lawn, walk the dog, fold the wash -- and let your mind wander over or away from the last five questions. You'll need to be refreshed to tackle the next two.

Getting Serious
6. What happens when someone joins your family?
7. What happens when someone leaves your family?

These questions help you look at the small and large transitions that occur in your family life. At the deepest level these are questions about birth and death and at the most superficial level they are about saying hello and good-bye. In workshops, we begin by describing intermediate transitions we have experienced ourselves: the first day of kindergarten and the last day of a school year or a summer camp experience. We think back to these and other changes we went through as children and young adults. Participants are encouraged to take time to reminisce

Questions, not Answers

with their kids and share these memories, both the lighter and often humorous ones, as well as more serious ones. In the workshops, as we consider these passages, we recall how we felt when they occurred.

Think of some beginnings ...remember your first day of kindergarten ...your first day in a new job or new school. Describe that experience using the conversational formula, "**I felt ___ about ___ because ___ .**" Now recall that experience again mentioning something you or someone else did that helped you feel secure. Again, try using the phrase, "**I felt ___ about ___ because ___ .**"

Then think of some endings ...your last day in grade school ...high school graduation ...the end of a summer camp. Consider the experience twice, first describing the so-called negative feelings (sadness, regret, fear, uncertainty) and then the more positive feelings (pleasure, pride, relief, sense of accomplishment). Often there's both an upside and downside to our more memorable experiences, and our attitudes strongly influence the effect of these experiences on us. If we look at the negative aspects of an experience and acknowledge the feelings these provoke, we can better see the positive aspects and more fully acknowledge and celebrate the good feelings these inspire.

From the first day of kindergarten through high school, college and new jobs, most of us wonder, "Will they like me? Can I do it? Will it be fun?" Recalling and acknowledging your own worries may help you to be more understanding of your child's present-day anxieties.

Deep emotions do come up in our workshops, of course. A participant in one of our early sessions described her grandmother's funeral, how desperate and lonely she felt at losing someone very, very dear and close to her. A participant in another workshop, recalling leaving her young daughter at day care, began crying. A father of preschoolers recalled his mother's recent death and was overcome with grief. Parents Forum facilitators acknowledge that participants may experience very strong feelings as they answer these questions and affirm that this is an important part of the process.

If a participant brings up a serious current issue, a facilitator may ask him or her if they want some feed-back or advice. When we give each other advice -- sometimes solutions to other peoples' problems are often easier to see than solutions to our own -- we try to present it, without pressure, in the form a question, "Have you considered...?" or "You might...." or "What about...?" We don't tell people what to do unless they specifically ask for suggestions (for example, sharing information about community resources) and generally we try to offer sympathy and empathy and share sto-ries about how we have dealt with similar challenges.

Discussing these two Getting Serious questions with family members or a trusted friend may help you anticipate your own needs when transitions loom. The stages of our children's lives can bring up feelings of sadness and happiness both, as we mourn in some way the loss of our little kid and delight in our child's passing a new milestone. More than one dad has held back or shed some tears as he sees his daughter in her first prom gown. More than a few mothers have found the first day of kindergarten to be the occasion of a 'crying club.'

Of course, there are beginnings and endings every day. You can think of these two questions as "How do you say hello?" and "How do you say good-bye?" In today's busy life we are constantly leaving one place and the people there and arriving at another place where we interact with other people. Even when we are in one place all day, we experience beginnings and endings to parts of the day. A workshop I attended on effective meetings stressed the importance of allowing time at the beginning and end of each meeting for social conversation. The "small talk" might be on weather, sports, movies or simply casual conversation, even the inconsequential "How have you been?" as a lead-in to the "big talk" of the meeting. The leader of that workshop gave several examples, describing all of our interactions -- telephone conversations, chance in-person encounters at the market, even e-mail message exchanges -- as meetings that can benefit from a courteous "lead-in" and "lead-out."

An uncommon courtesy, one I appreciate when others offer it to me, is asking, especially when calling on the telephone, "Is this a good time?" I try to remember to ask this of others. When people of any age, children or adults, are given this choice they can usually listen more attentively. If we pay attention to the small transitions in our lives and try to make them with some grace, we may find it easier to meet the greater transitions we inevitably face in a similar manner.

Now, we move on to the last question.

Stating Changes
8. What changes have you experienced recently?
    What changes do you expect in the future?

The workshops close with a discussion of change and this is a two-in-one question, looking back, then forward. It is inevitable, of course. Becoming a parent, becoming a successful parent, means learning to deal with change and teaching our children to do so as

well. There are all kinds of changes in our lives:
changes in ourselves, those in others, changes we
anticipate with delight, those we dread, changes we
share and those we accomplish or suffer alone. People
change at different rates and sometimes the changes
we make take us in different directions. An awareness
of values, a sense of the values we hold most dear can
be a life preserver in a sea of change.

The importance of the changes we experience in our
lives becomes clear if we first recognize them, then talk
about them, and celebrate or lament them. We do this
in our workshops and one
special thing we do is to
celebrate the end of each
Parents Forum workshop as
a graduation. We give certificates to everyone who has
participated and we ask each
person to give their own mini-
valedictory on the topic of change.

Each of us wants to do a good job as a parent. We
want to be happy and want the same for our spouse
or partner, our parents, siblings, children and our

*A newspaper reporter attended a one-day workshop,
intending to sit outside the circle, observe and write
about the process. We invited him to sit in, instead.
Although not a parent himself, he spent the next several hours enthusiastically sharing his own experiences, thoughts and feelings, listening to others, commenting on the roleplays and finally giving his own
short graduation speech. His perspectives on parenting, as a recent 'consumer' of parent 'services' were
helpful to the parents of young children. His participation enriched the discussion for all of us.*

bosses and coworkers too. If we fully experience the changes we have to make in the course of our lives, and if we accept and manage in positive ways the anger, fear and sadness that come up along the way, we can more fully enjoy the happiness that life brings. A friend told me once that "Sorrow carves out so that joy may fill up."

The practices described above: considering feelings and thoughts and discussing them with other parents, along with asking these eight key questions, are the foundations of Parents Forum . They help us see the shifting, sometimes fuzzy line between cherishing our children (good for them and for us) and coddling them (often not so good either for them or for us).

These practices are useful whether you have an infant, a teenager, children grown and gone or, perhaps, adult children living with you (or you are living with them) because of economic or other necessity. The practices can be useful whether you live in a big city, a town or open country, no matter what world you live in: New or Old, North or South, no matter whether you live in a developed or a developing country. Thoughtful, caring and mutually supportive discussions with other parents help us become better guides for our children as they grow, grow up and perhaps go on to create their own families.

Watch Your Words and
Your Silences

Chapter Six

Watch Your Words

As parents, we risk passing along to our children the tension that we experience and we can, all too easily, let our kids' moods affect us as well. Patience wearing thin, a mother swears at her kids to "clean up the (expletive) playroom." With five minutes to go before the school bus arrives, another mom berates her daughter for misplacing her backpack, "What's wrong with you? Are you a dummy?" This chapter focuses on how we behave towards our children when we are tired, anxious, angry -- or all three -- and how we behave toward them when they are tired, anxious or angry. It suggests conversational safety valves that kids and parents alike can use.

It should be noted that our silences, like our words, deserve our attention, too. How many of us can remember, as children, talking to one of our parents and having mom or dad say, "I'm listening, go ahead..." without looking up from a newspaper or a cookbook? Can you remember how you felt? Unheard? Unconsidered? Unimportant?

With the stresses most parents experience, most of us have done this, at one time or another, with our children, spouse or partner. "Sure, sweetheart, I hear you," we may say when we're only half listening. We have good intentions. We start to listen, or may look as if we're listening, but in reality we're just waiting for the other person to stop talking so we can go back to whatever we were doing. "Using our words" both honestly and lovingly is half the work in building and maintaining any relationship; listening attentively is the other half.

Mastery of these crucial skills requires empathy, a quality defined in the dictionary as an "understanding of the situation, feelings and motives of another person." Imagine that each of us is born with our own internal "empathy account," and to the extent that others and we ourselves "make deposits" to this account we are able to "draw" on our reserves and extend empathy to others. Parents especially, who are called on daily to give good attention and understanding to their children, need to receive the same in order to maintain their "accounts." If family members or friends, in Parents Forum or another supportive setting, listen to me without judging me when I need to talk about my worries and challenges, I will probably be better able to listen to my children. This talking and listening helps raise our emotional awareness. Emotional awareness, in turn, helps us deal with the strong feelings -- and impulses -- that come up in the course of family life. In Parents Forum, we develop our emotional awareness with exercises using both active and passive communications skills: we practice expressing our own feelings and practice listening attentively to others express theirs.

Suppose that the two mothers described at the beginning of this chapter could, later, share with each other their disappointment in themselves at their angry and sarcastic outbursts. They could recall, too, the many caring and considerate moments they've had with their children. Maybe each could find a reasonably unstressed time to talk with her kids, to apologize and to ask for suggestions on how, as a family, they could avoid such blowups. Maybe these two moms could discuss the conflicts they each anticipate and agree to speak again afterwards, using the "bookend" technique described in Chapter 5.

When parents own up to their mistakes, they model this behavior for their children. Apologizing is a crucial step in improving family communication. However, an apology alone may be insufficient. A parent screams, apologizes, screams, apologizes. A teen breaks curfew, apologizes, breaks curfew again, and so on. An automatic or "pro forma" apology, one made without reflecting on the circumstances or motives leading up to the event that prompted it, may simply be a stepping stone in a circular path leading back to hurting a loved one again. You may notice such a pattern in your home. If you do, you can discuss that pattern and consider how to change it. Both participants may see changes they can make. Most of the time, it does "take two to tangle."

In a workshop, when parents describe an argument or confrontation, we find it helpful to recall the agenda questions four and five, about values and rules. How do your values determine the household rules regarding parents speaking with each other? Does my behavior (yelling, name-calling, swearing) violate those rules? Are rules for parent-to-parent discussion and conflict the same as those for parent-to-child and child-to-parent conversation and argument?

Are certain words not permitted? What sorts of expression are allowed, encouraged or forbidden when feelings run high? Are children encouraged to cry if they feel like it? What about adults? Can we cry too? Who sulks and for how long, usually? Are there time limits for arguments and silences, for discussing and not discussing problems? What do you say and what helps you "watch your words"? How do you know if you are really listening or being listened to? Do you turn off the radio, the television, the computer so that you can hear and be heard?

As difficult as it is to do everything we need to do in a day, it is sometimes even harder, at home, to take time to be kind and to make time to listen. We want to "let our hair down" and be able to let our defenses down. But this can be dangerous in a stressful situation. The latitude we both need and expect at home can lead to hurtful lapses in the way we speak to the people we live with.

Don't family members deserve the same courtesy we
show to people outside our homes? Don't relatives and
friends deserve from us the kind of attention we'd like
to receive from them? Still, most of us have moments
when it is hard to resist the temptation to "come home
and kick the dog" to relieve frustrations we've experienced during the workday. Our goal in Parents Forum
is to develop practices of diffusing tensions before they
get the better of us, or rather, before they bring out
the worst in us! We can teach our kids appropriate
ways to deal with their frustrations by not giving them
a "dog-kicking" role model. This is much easier to do if
we take time to put some guidelines in place.

Family rules can spell out some ways to deal with
these difficulties. For example, maybe a few minutes
of quiet time after coming in the door will help each of
us make a "gentle landing" after a busy day. If you find
yourself "facing off" with your cranky five-year-old or
your exhausted spouse, take a deep breath, listen as
attentively as you can and then use words that you
would like to hear if you were in your child's or partner's place: "What's the matter?" "Shall I just listen?"
"Is there something I can do to help?" However, if you
can't give them good attention, be honest about that:
"This isn't a good time, could we talk later?" Be specific and then keep your promise. Perhaps set the timer
for a brief period -- this might be a good tactic with a
preschooler. You could say "Dad (or Mom) needs a time
out." Or, for a larger issue or a longer delay, write a
note and put it on the refrigerator, or give your spouse
or child an IOU ("I owe you") for listening.

Of course, when feelings run high they demand attention. My anger or my angry kid cannot be "shelved"
indefinitely. Many cultures, including our own in
North America, lack adequate support for expressing
powerful negative feelings in a way that doesn't harm
others. Parents Forum is one of a number of programs

striving to remedy this lack. It is true that expressing feelings at the wrong times, or in the wrong ways, can damage our relationships with people we care about. But emotions fuel our behaviors and failing to take time to recognize and channel or express them can do serious damage to our own and others' well-being. If we put thought in the driver's seat, even strong negative feelings can be expressed in ways that minimize harm. Change is possible, although it does take practice and time to develop new patterns of behavior. We can learn to advocate for our own emotional needs and teach our children to do the same.

Speaking sharply to children is one thing. Sometimes you have to raise your voice to get their attention. Or if you have been yelling a lot, lower your voice. A change, in and of itself, may get attention. Choose your words carefully and try using the conversational formula: "I feel extremely frustrated and upset about your leaving the living room a mess because we're having company soon and I want this place to look nice!" Raising your voice in this instance can produce a desired result without causing harm. Shaming or humiliating words, on the other hand ("What the 'bleep' is the matter with you kids? You left this place a pigsty!"), whether they are spoken quietly or hurled full force, can be as damaging as a physical blow.

There was one moment when I knew I had made significant progress in becoming a calmer, more reasonable and more effective parent. Michael, my youngest, was five or six years old. His brother Luke, a teenager, had committed some misdeed. Michael, seeing my evident anger, advised me, "Mom, you'll have to speak sharply to Luke." If speaking sharply was the ultimate sanction, I had really made progress!

The rhyme, "Sticks and stones may break my bones, but words will never hurt me" might more accurately read, "Sticks and stones can break my bones and words can break my spirit." If the conver-  sational climate in your home is more often stormy than sunny, if you or your kids yell a lot, and you would like to change this, you can. Just as walking every day gradually tones your body, working daily to raise your emotional awareness can increase your peace of mind and the harmony in your household.

As I became aware of the damage that blaming and shaming language caused, I vowed to make changes in how I spoke to my boys. This was so difficult that I felt I was practically learning a new language. A key element in my re-education was the acceptance and support I received from other parents. They gently encouraged me to be honest about what had gone on and what was still going on in my family and loved me anyway, even though a lot of it wasn't pretty. Their gentleness with me helped me become more gentle with myself.

I write this as a parent, happy now to have peace- ful relations, for the most part, with my grown sons. Let me share a young person's perspective. A friend of mine, a young woman about thirty years old, still suffers from her mother's unrelenting criti- cism. My friend said she finds it difficult to visit her family home, because everyone is so negative. She said she recently realized that, as a child, "I thought my mother hated me because she was so hateful to me."

In one intense parent weekend in the treatment program, the counselor leading the session asked each parent in the group to stand, in turn, and describe an incident where we had behaved in a way we later regretted. When my turn came, I remember crying as I described a time when I had hit one of my boys with uncontrolled anger. I remember the loving attention of the group and the parents sitting next to me holding my hands as I spoke. Saying out loud how I had hurt my son relieved the hurt -- from that incident and others -- hurt I had been holding inside. At that moment their warmth and understanding allowed me to forgive myself and I realized I could change.

Gradually I developed more patience with my children. While I tried to be more honest with myself and with them about my feelings, I tried just as hard to consider their feelings and possible reactions. Our household rules, posted on the refrigerator, began with a few lines about our values (a family "mission statement" you could call it) and continued with a list of do's and don'ts in various categories. Consequences for not following the rules (one particularly dreaded punishment was "no grilled cheese sandwiches") were spelled out too. The rules have been through many revisions, starting out short, getting longer and then shorter again once my boys moved out. Over twenty years later, our rules are still posted. Learning to be both patient and honest is a challenge and, even with clear rules in plain sight, it is easy to get sidetracked. It takes time but we all can change.

Another technique that can be helpful is keeping a personal journal. I still find this a useful discipline when I face some difficult situation because it gives me a clear starting point for my efforts to change. Try keeping a journal or a brief log for a few days or a week to monitor the verbal "weather" in your home.

Each evening, for several days at least, take ten or fifteen minutes to write down one or two significant exchanges that took place during the day. You can do this writing exercise alone or, if your spouse or partner is willing, you can do it with him or her or with another family member. Consider how adults and children in your family speak to each other. The observation and comment should be gentle, of course, otherwise the cure could be worse than the complaint. Notice whether you repeatedly make light of each other's concerns. Do you try to convince family members that they don't really feel what they say they feel? Do you ignore each other? When one family member asks for support does another ask for the same, a kind of "one-up" game? Do people change the subject or interrupt each other frequently? Notes, if you take them, are best used to promote discussion and resolution of conflicts. Using them to support attacks and accusations defeats the purpose.

If writing seems too formal, or if a family member is unwilling to join you in this evaluation, you could make a telephone appointment with a friend and complete the exercise, over a few days' time, in conversation. Another person's perspective may be helpful. Referring to the questions from the Parents Forum agenda may put your conversations (or arguments) in a clearer light as you consider, "Was that a Question 2 issue, about concern?" "...a Question 4 issue, about values?" "...a Question 7 issue, about saying goodbye?"

Perspectives differ, of course: I might feel terribly regretful at having lost my temper or terribly hurt at something my husband or son said. But after talking with him I might find, to my surprise, that he remembered neither incident!

A helpful reference is *The Verbally Abusive Relationship*, by Patricia Evans. It suggests patterns of speech that signal possible abusiveness and lists behaviors that go beyond simple yelling, such as withholding praise or accidentally-on-purpose "forgetting" about a promise to take a child to the movies, for example. Rather than worry excessively about real or imagined verbal abuse I suffered or inflicted, I now try to consider any hurtful exchange of words and talk it over with a friend. Whether my words hurt someone else or their words hurt me, it helps to talk about what happened with a third party. Identifying a problem is the first step toward remedying it. Try not to be too hard on yourself or family members. One incident of discounting a child's pain or one broken promise of a trip to the park does not establish a pattern. What counts is the overall consistent emotional climate of our family lives.

Even in giving care, we can unthinkingly disrespect a child's feelings. A four-year-old falls, scrapes his knee and comes crying into the kitchen. Mom says, "Oh, don't be silly. Don't make such a fuss " She didn't hit him. She cleaned and bandaged his knee. But she also trivialized his feelings. As an isolated incident, such an exchange may not qualify as abuse. Repeated over time, however, such comments could set a child up to discount his or her own feelings as well as the feelings of playmates. If we consistently minimize our chil-

> *Well-intentioned parents -- I count myself one -- can discourage a child. A sixth-grader's report card has A's in four subjects and a C in history. Instead of a big smile and, "I see you really worked hard this term!" Mom or Dad says, "What happened with your history grade?" One of my sons told me that he hated my saying, "Good effort!" because he heard it as, "You made a good effort but you came up short." I'm glad he told me. I stopped saying that.*

dren's sadness, hurt or fear, they learn that these feelings are not important to us. A child then, perhaps
deliberately or unconsciously, suppresses his feelings
and in the process becomes less able to empathize
with others.

In popular magazines, I've read several articles on the
topic of bullying that say children may provoke in others the feelings they are discouraged from expressing
themselves. For example, a child who is not allowed to
show he is afraid, or who is ridiculed for showing fear,
might try to intimidate other children. In trying to get
our children to be "strong" or "tough" when physically
or emotionally hurt -- before they're done experiencing
and expressing their pain or disappointment -- we may
be setting a pattern of disrespect for other people's
feelings.

Watching our words and silences is not something
many of us do naturally. But if we devote time to helping our children develop patience and understanding,
 just as we do to teaching them how
to read and count, to identify colors
and to ride a bike, they will acquire
these qualities.

Apologizing doesn't come easily for
many of us. It can be difficult, even
uncomfortable, to say, "I'm sorry,"
especially if the phrase has not
been part of your vocabulary in the
past. One of the lessons of recovery that I find especially useful at times I've made mistakes is to keep my
apology "brief, blunt and to the point." I try to say just
one thing, "sorry," perhaps using, "**I feel** sorry **about
___ because ___** ," without looking back and justify-
ing my mistake or looking forward and anticipating the
other person's response. If the situation is one that
has happened before or that is likely to recur, I may,

> *At a class reunion some years ago, I met a high school friend and her husband and, as is common at such gatherings, we shared parenting "war stories." One of these offers a unique safety-valve tactic. Judy and Jack Palmer described how they would sit on the floor in a circle with their daughter and her preschool friends (the friends' parents too, sometimes), everyone with a pillow in their lap. Each person had a chance to tell the others what they were mad about and why. A kid, hitting her pillow, might say, "Take that, Mom, on the lips, for calling me a dope!" Mom would respond by holding her hands to her mouth and yelling, "Owwwww, that hurts!" Around the circle, Dad, hitting the pillow in his lap, might*

as a reminder to myself as much as a signal to the other person, state a change I will make. Still, simpler is usually better.

Apologizing means taking a risk. The person receiving the apology may interpret the expression of regret as an opening for an attack. It is helpful if family rules are clear on how apologies are made and accepted. Apology, like praise, is best when it's genuine, unforced and focused. If I've screamed at my child, I could say, "I'm sorry for yelling and I see you look upset. I am completely out of patience. I feel very frustrated because you still haven't put away your building blocks!" Then take a breath, and consider next steps, both words and action.

As parents, we can make an effort to become conscious of the quality of our speaking and our listening right from the beginning. The concern here is not about an occasional tantrum or argument, but the overall day-in and day-out emotional and conversational climate in your home. Judgment about the seriousness of distress is yours to make. Reasonable people disagree, usually with a degree of calm.

say, "Take that, Jamie, on the hand, for knocking over the milk!" and Jamie would squeeze his hands together, crying out loud, "Ouuuuuch!" Mom's accusation, "Take that, Nancy, on the ear, for not listening to me about hanging up your clothes!" would provoke an, "Oh no, my ear, that hurts too much!" from Nancy. The game was a big success with neighborhood children who would come over and ask to play. I should emphasize that this game is not about trivializing physical abuse. Done in the right spirit, it can effectively relieve tension. As Judy and Jack described the game, feelings were heard, no one was hit and the honesty and laughter of "Take That!" refreshed everyone.

Unreasonable people disagree too, usually unreasonably. The trick, worth learning, is how to talk calmly about provocative issues and behaviors. It can be done.

Is your family's conversational style generally dismissive? Is it manipulative? Is it competitive -- do speakers not acknowledge each other or try to dominate each other? Or is it combative, with frequent or long-running arguments? If you recognize these patterns, do you want to change them? If impatience or disrespect is chronic and ingrained in one or more family members, it is unlikely that family harmony will burst out, like sun from behind the clouds, overnight.

If one person makes a change, however small, other family members will sooner or later respond. The person who wants to initiate a positive change may benefit from focused self-help programs and/or professional counseling. If there are questions about the mental health or physical safety of a family member, obviously, seek help without delay. At the very least, seek advice about getting help. If reading this chapter has made you uncomfortable, take the discomfort as

a caution light, and slow down. The next time you feel
angry, tired or sad, remember to breathe. Call or sit
with someone and talk, cry or laugh (maybe all three)
about whatever is upsetting you. Let your anger,
fatigue and sadness out. But even the most caring
friend may not be able to give you the support you
need. There are many reasons why parents lose
patience and speak or behave in ways that distress
or damage their children.

Our program cannot take the place of professional
counseling. Some problems may go beyond normal
range or continue for an extended period. If your family history includes any known or suspected incidence
of anxiety, depression, eating disorders, suicidality or
other mental illness, alcoholism or trauma, please
seek guidance from professionals who have experience
treating those conditions. Don't wait for a crisis.

Parent peer support, as wonderful as it is, has limits.
But what can it do? In a nutshell, we see our program,
and others like it, offering parents opportunities to dis-
tinguish between small, insignificant problems and
small, potentially serious ones. Some parents make
mountains out of molehills and in so doing create un-
warranted distress for themselves and their children.
Other parents ignore warning signs that, if heeded,
can lead them get help and avoid serious problems.

Exciting research in the fields of brain development
and communications may offer insights into how peer
support works. Scientific study is not our expertise
but we hope to find a research partner interested in
our work and discover why Parents Forum participants give us such consistently favorable feedback.

Raising Parents

Chapter Seven

Raising Parents

Children make their needs clear, "Feed me... love me... teach me... play with me... help me find my way in the world...." These needs recall the handy guide presented in Chapter Four and they do, in fact, persist into adulthood. As parents we want to meet our children's needs and we'll have a better chance of doing so if we acknowledge and address our own needs as well. In effect, parents need raising too! We need different kinds of support at different stages of our own and our children's development. Teen parents may need more help than a couple in their 20s or 30s. A first-time mother needs a different sort of assistance than a mother having her second or third baby. The challenge we sought to meet in founding Parents Forum was to create an organization open enough and flexible enough for parents and others at all stages of life to give and get needed support for family life.

This chapter describes the steps we took in developing Parents Forum in Cambridge and Somerville, Massachusetts. Our plan and practices may suggest steps you can take to organize Parents Forum in your community. Please see the note at the end of the book regarding use of the Parents Forum program and name and contact us.

In 1994, shortly after we organized our first Parents Forum workshops, we learned that the United Nations had designated that year as the International Year of the Family. For us the timing could not have been better as it offered a broader context for our efforts. The U.N. declaration read, in part, *"Changes in our society [have] much affected and altered the family...[However] the family is a powerful agent for social, political, economic and cultural change and a potential vehicle for development. The family must be given assistance and -- if need be -- protection, so that it can fully assume its responsibilities as the basic unit of society."*

These encouraging words helped us move forward. We realized that the struggles we faced were not unique and, more importantly, we saw that we could take action to "fully assume our responsibilities" as parents. From our own experiences we had learned the benefit of mutual support, but how could we get other parents involved?

At first, we decided Parents Forum events would be free to individuals but we do now accept donations from participants if the host agency allows. We felt that businesses, schools and other public and private agencies would support our activities through sponsorship and fees in order to foster healthy family life and create stronger communities. We offered prizes as incentives for parents to come and we hold prize drawings both during and at the end of events to encourage parents to stay involved. Fundraising remains a significate challenge.

Discussions in the first few years got stuck several times on the question of professional versus non-professional leadership. We eventually chose volunteers leaders because we believe our Tools of the Trade and our Agenda of eight questions offer an accessible and adaptable, low-tech curriculum that non-professionals can use successfully in leading group discussions. We avoid unsolicited advice-giving in the workshops. The reason for this is to blur, if not erase, the line between those giving help and those receiving it. A suggestion for solving a problem may be what someone needs, but he or she is more likely to accept it if they have asked for it. The suggestion may meet with less resistance, too, if it is presented as one option rather than the one "right answer."

Workshop facilitators model empathetic listening and share their own struggles, before giving any advice. Often participants and facilitators tell each other about community resources and both benefit from the exchange.

We wanted volunteer workshop leaders to act as facilitators, not experts, in order to honor parents' leadership in their families. Many counselors, mental health care providers and parenting education specialists recognize the value of mutual help as prevention or as follow-up to professional help. They and others encouraged our efforts. Still, we had a lot to do when we began "raising" our program, as the idea of positive mutual support for parents was new. We had to promote and develop our program at the same time.

One of the coordinators of our first spin-off group described what she got from Parents Forum when she volunteered to come to our local community television station to be filmed for a public service announcement. I had no idea what she would say but I shouldn't have worried. "I learned," she said, "that the most important thing I can give my kids is creativity and I don't need to give them so much stuff." She described how she had gotten help cleaning and straightening her children's playroom, how she had called on other Parents Forum participants to baby-sit occasionally and how she had organized a number of community events for other parents. She mentioned how she'd had fun, too, and how much it meant to her to be able to help others. She and her husband had developed their leadership skills and self-confidence to the point that they had agreed to co-chair their school's Parent Teacher Association.

Here are the elements needed to create Parents Forum in your community:

- people to organize the activities and to seek community involvement from others: coordinator(s), workshop facilitator(s), treasurer, writer or publicist, secretary and other volunteers

- people to participate: parents and others of all ages, and partner agencies, especially parent groups

- sponsors: librarians and literacy advocates, educators, public health agencies, business people, service clubs, artists, athletes and sports clubs, journalists (print, broadcast, and cable and electronic media), to provide financial support and offer prizes

- agencies serving families in need as beneficiaries of the surplus goods donated in book and toy exchanges

- prizes for participants: goods and gift certificates for goods and services useful to families -- this includes the basics (food and clothing) as well as museum passes, tickets to movie theaters and sports events and vouchers for classes for children or adults and so on

- hosts to offer places to meet: library, cultural center, workplace, school, clinic, church, temple or mosque

- people to lead activities for children and teens and to provide childcare at meetings

- refreshments (remember, "Feed me!")

• and, last but not least, organized
activities, including the workshops described in previous
chapters as well as several other
activities described below.

To begin, get a small group of
people together and take an
inventory of your needs and skills.
What sorts of activities will you
organize and when? Who is willing
to take the lead? Who will come to your events and
how will you contact and attract them? Who will ask
for donations and keep track of expenditures? Who
will call or visit prospective hosts and sponsors?
Will some of the people involved receive stipends for
their work?

A note or two on fundraising is in order at this point,
as asking for donations can be difficult for many people. The best I can say about fundraising is that as difficult as it may be at the outset, it gets easier each
time you do it. When you approach a friend, associate
or business person for money, you are, of course, asking for something, but you are also offering something
important in return. You are offering prospective
donors a chance to make a difference in their community. If you use the skills you developed and practiced
in Chapter Five, these conversations become easier. If
the plan for your activity is clear, if the benefit to families in your community is evident and, most important, if you are convinced of its value, you are very
likely to receive the donation or support you request.
Of course, some people will still say NO, but they may
be able to offer assistance another time or may give
you valuable advice on other sources of support.

In addition to seeking donations, Parents Forum requests fees for its services from host agencies or licenses the curriculum to them, training volunteers from the host agency. Established groups, like PTA or PTO and parent discussion groups at clinics or shelters, are ideal hosts for Parents Forum, as are college and university family weekend programs. Community-based family resource centers and work/life programs offered by employers can incorporate Parents Forum into their offerings. Some companies have corporate social responsibility initiatives that can involve employees in helping organize a Book and Toy Exchange or, with preparation, can send volunteers to give Parents Forum workshops in prisons as part of reentry/reintegration programming.

A book and toy exchange, with planning and publicity efforts usually beginning three months in advance, can take place in a library or community center from 11:00 to 1:00 on a Saturday. The library or another agency donates the space and announces the event in its calendars. Volunteer coordinators send announcements to schools, home-schooling families, faith communities and newspapers and they solicit prizes and

refreshments from local businesses. Parents Forum
reaches out to all segments of the community, including public, parochial and private school families as
well as home-schoolers.

During the ten days before the announced date, people
drop off their donations at branch libraries. Donations
are also accepted on the day of the Book and Toy
Exchange. We especially request books on parenting
and family life and we ask local agencies to send literature about their programs for parents and families.
Then it happens: Coordinators and volunteers who
agreed to help come to the designated location and
organize the donated items by age group. People come
with their kids -- we have a table with art activities for
the children -- and parents and children freely give
and take the books and toys that have been set out.
Door prizes are drawn mid-way through the exchange
and at the end. A local charity -- a shelter or youth
center, for example -- receives the books and toys
remaining at the end of the two hours. In choosing a
homeless shelter, for example, as the beneficiary of a
Book and Toy Exchange, Parents Forum recognizes
and responds to peoples' desire to help others who
are experiencing greater need.

*At the Parents Forum Book & Toy Exchange in October
2000 at the Cambridge (Mass.) Public Library, Susana,
from Argentina and Cambridge, mother of Markie,
age 2 1/2, said, "Great job! Do it again!" Igor,
a World Boston Community Connections visitor from
Vyborg, near St. Petersburg, and the father of Slavik,
six years old, commented, "We have nothing like this in
Russia. So many people, everyone is so interested, and
everybody needs it, this bring and take." "Fantastic! I
saw the flyer in the library . . . I couldn't resist. I have
a big bag of books and I'm still looking," added Ceane,*

Volunteers at the event screen the donations, sort them and keep the tables in order during the two-hour exchange. Book and Toy Exchanges offer a respite from the materialism and commercialism that seem to have ever greater sway in our society. For two hours people give what they can and take what they need without money changing hands. Parents have a chance to teach their children about charity, "We'll give away this book you no longer enjoy. What would you like to take? [and] Leave some things for others to take, too." The exchange of books and toys mirrors the exchange of insights and experiences that takes place in our conversations. Parents make new friends at these events and are able to pick up brochures about local resources for families.

Another successful Parents Forum activity, Playroom Makeovers, grew out of an informal planning meeting when the hosting parent, acknowledging the clutter of toys, admitted, "I went overboard last Christmas." We made an appointment for a two-hour session one evening and together sorted through puzzles, trucks, dolls and blocks. Some items were clearly ready to be discarded or given away. Others were set aside for when their children were a little older. We designated a

mother of Zoe, 2 1/2 years old, from Charlestown. At the end of the two-hour free event more than a dozen bags of books and toys remained for the beneficiary of the event, a family shelter in Boston for people recovering from alcohol and other drug abuse. Door prizes included gift certificates from restaurants and career consultants. Like the other Book and Toy Exchanges held in Cambridge and Somerville, this one elicited favorable comments from a social worker and therapist who attended, "Parents need this and it would be great if you offer regular groups."

place for every kind of toy. The result was a clean play-room and, while it may not have stayed that way for long, the order we created was uplifting for both parents and kids. It served as a reference point and an inspiration for regular playroom clean-up. It gave us an opportunity to socialize while doing something useful. This activity illustrates, too, the way Parents Forum coordinators can develop new ideas on their own.

Several mini-workshops have evolved through participation in community events organized by other agencies. The first is Telling Our Own Stories, where we set up a display table with our program literature at a fair or other community event. We engage parents, with their children, in conversation, asking them to reminisce about happy family events -- basically answering the first agenda question "What do you like about your family?" This mini-workshop can serve as volunteer training, with individual volunteers serving for an hour at the table to get experience talking informally with new people, without the pressure of standing up in front of a group. This activity can be done, too, as an art activity for children alone, or while parents are involved in workshop discussions.

> *At Family Fun Day, an annual Cambridge Family Literacy Collaborative event, we once invited parents and children to cut out a hand shape and write on it the name of their favorite book, adding each favorite book to a poster as the day went along. Another year we invited fair-goers to talk about their family experiences. An elder volunteering at the event told a story about her many years as a foster parent, proudly emphasizing that all the children who came to her finished high school. People love to share their stories and have too few opportunities to do so.*

Another mini-workshop is based on our third agenda
question is called How To Tell Somebody Something
They'd Rather Not Hear (HTTSSTRNH), and was developed as part of Charm School at the Massachusetts
Institute of Technology. This event, a four-hour "manners fair," is presented on the MIT campus each
January. You might be surprised at a science and
engineering university venturing into the etiquette
business, but the event is a great success and has
gotten national media coverage. There are booths
on table manners and how to make introductions,
demonstrations of ballroom dancing, "elevator etiquette," role-plays on asking for a date, library manners, presentations on telephone manners, effective
e-mail and how to write social correspondence.

At the Parents Forum booth, HTTSSTRNH, volunteer
faculty-for-a-day discuss troublesome situations
described by people who join us for a 15-minute session. We cover a variety of sticky situations: firing
somebody or quitting a job, telling a student she or
he didn't pass an exam, breaking up with a boyfriend
or girlfriend, confronting somebody about their heavy
drinking. Even minor confrontations, like re-claiming
one's place in line if someone has cut in front of you,
come up. Following the Parents Forum protocol, we
do brief roleplays using the conversational formula
"I feel _____ about _____ because _____."

The groups are small, usually ten or twelve people and
roleplay participants leave with new strategies and
energy for addressing challenging situations in their
personal and academic lives. Those who do not take
part in a roleplay still learn a useful lesson when they
see that sticky situations -- and life is full of them --
can be more successfully handled if uncomfortable
feelings are addressed.

Raising Parents

Parents Forum can be presented in 20 minutes or two and a half hours. The long workshop presenting all eight questions is "I.T. for Parents: Insights and tools for parenting with less stress." Each mini-workshop "Telling Our Own Stories," "Becoming the Parent Your College Kid Needs" and "How To Tell Somebody Something They'd Rather Not Hear" takes less time but still presents the essential elements of the program. "Book and Toy Exchanges" and "Playroom Makeovers" provide practical support. All these activities can support us as we strive to meet the enormous demands of family and society. Wherever we live, we have similar hopes for our children. We also need similar kinds of support if we are to provide for their wellbeing and assure their healthy development.

In Parents Forum, we believe that there are a few general requirements for a successful parents program. They should be free (or with modest donations requested), frequent and fun, must solicit parents' feedback and must serve refreshments. We call these "the five F's." We also ask workshop hosts to provide childcare, as the cost of a baby-sitter or the inconvenience of leaving a child at home can discourage parents from attending. If you plan to organize your own Parents Forum, it is important also to consider the "five W's" of parenting education:

WHAT is parenting education? Practical skills coupled with knowledge about child and adolescent development and about parenting "best practices."

WHO offers parenting education? Many people in parents' lives teach us, or can teach us, important lessons, among them medical and mental health care providers and ordinary folks including our own parents, friends and neighbors. WHO pays? Public and private agencies and community-minded businesses;

114

parents themselves may also pay for courses or professionally led seminars.

WHERE does parenting education happen? Lots of places, from formal settings like classrooms to informal ones like the bleachers at a ball game.

WHEN does it happen? Not often enough! Kindergarten was once an innovation. Now it's part of almost all school programs. We want to put parents' concerns on the policy agenda of government, business and civil society and we see universally accessible parenting education as our long-term goal.

WHY is parenting education important? The cost of parents being ill-prepared to raise children is borne by all of us, personally and socially.

How can we better prepare to feed... love... teach... play with... and help our children find their way in the world? We need to take time to prepare, but how can we find the time when so many of our daily tasks are not optional? A crying baby needs to be fed, changed or soothed. Toddlers need to be picked up or dropped off at daycare. Preschoolers need an art activity or a trip to the park. A school-age child needs a hug, or homework checked or a story read. A teen or young adult child needs advice (seldom), needs a ride somewhere (often) or needs money (still more often!) A supervisor insists on a report or a customer needs an order by the end of the day. An appliance signals (the microwave beeps, the clothes dryer buzzes) calling our attention. We are lucky to have them, of course -- the kids, the work and the conveniences -- but taking breaks between urgent tasks is as essential as the tasks themselves. We also need food, friendship, information and skills, fun times and a chance to become involved in our community. Parents Forum and other programs for parents play an essential role in community life. Businesses and community agencies can help by recognizing parenting education as a cornerstone of family support.

The United Nations International Year of the Family, celebration in 1994, had as its emblem a heart enfolding a heart under a roof and its theme was "family is the smallest democracy at the heart of society."

In Parents Forum, we develop our ability to resolve conflicts respectfully (if not always democratically) and we focus on our capacity to give each other and our children intelligent and caring attention.

Each year May 15 is celebrated as International Day of Families with activities at the U.N. and in regional, national and local agencies. Your community can do the same. We try to "dwell in a place of abundance" even under constraints in material circumstances and under pressure of time. Parents, especially parents of young children, have too little of the latter. Giving our children and each other good attention during the moments we are together is a priceless gift.

Love and Order

Chapter Eight

Love and Order

Some years ago a couple involved in Parent Forum invited me over for a visit. We were sitting at the kitchen table when their almost six-year-old son sidled up to his mother. As he climbed into her lap, she said, "Why don't we ask Eve that question you asked me earlier?" and, with some encouragement, he asked, "Why are there big people who are mean?"

His mother told me she'd replied, "There are more good people than bad people in the world, but there still are some just plain mean folks." She was right, of course. The world is imperfect and people are imperfect. The underlying question I heard in her son's words, however, was, "How do people get to be mean?"

So, to my friend's response I added that I thought big people who are mean probably had parents who were mean to them when they were little. As we talked, I wondered aloud how mean parents probably punished their children harshly and weren't very loving. I recalled the Parents Forum workshop lesson on thoughts and feelings. In that lesson we considered our behavior from the perspective of thoughts: how we keep order in our households, and from the perspective of feelings: how we express affection. Mean parents may establish too little order (or enforce it too harshly) and may give too little love (or show it inconsistently). Effective parents provide adequate measures

Near the end of a long stay-at-home day when my boys were little, I recall one of them nagging me for more cookies. These happened to be lemon-flavored cookies. Frustrated, I yelled, "There have to be limits!" and, confusing lemons with limits he replied, "I want more limits!" If only kids were this clear all the time. They need our love, and cookies sometimes, but they need order too, and limits on the cookies.

118

of both order and love. Love and order. That sounds oh-so-simple, but giving our kids enough of both and achieving a balance between the two on a day-to-day, sometimes minute-to-minute basis, can be difficult indeed.

When we are new parents, our lives are completely taken up with the baby. As parents of school kids, then parents of young adults, we learn to do less as our children learn to do more for themselves. Only by taking breaks now and then from the day-to-day work of raising children can we get the perspective we need on their progress and on our own.

> *Babies need immediate and nearly constant atten-*
> *tion. A new father said, "There's no give and take.*
> *We give. He takes! It's total slavery." But he said*
> *this with a smile, knowing that as time passes there*
> *will be moments, and then longer and longer peri-*
> *ods, when he can expect his son to wait. Just not*
> *now -- the baby is only six months old.*

Our children always need our love, but they may want it expressed differently at different stages. Similarly, they need us to provide order in their lives in different ways at different ages. How can we judge whether we are doing a good job? To "keep tabs" on the balance of love and order in our parenting, we can benefit from reassurance, support and information from other adults. The order of these three elements is important: first, emotional reassurance, then practical support, and, finally, objective information. If the information the other person offers -- in whatever guise, either advice or instruction -- comes first, it may create a logjam, only increasing the frustration a parent feels from lack of either reassurance or support or both.

Love and Order

Think back to the exercise on expressing concern in "Tools of the Trade" where you used the formula **"I feel___ about___ because ___"** Remember that the feeling word comes first. Saying how you feel can, sometimes almost literally, take a "load off your chest." Describing the situation that caused the feeling can be a relief too. Even better is getting help with the situation.

Note that, while Parents Forum does not offer specific services, as participants get to know one another and become friends, they may help each other out with childcare, housework, finances and that all important referral: the name of a dependable plumber.

After dealing with the two elements, reassurance and practical support, we can talk about the whys and wherefores and get the information we need to understand the situation and the feelings it brought up. Keeping these three elements in order, especially the part about monitoring our own feelings, is essential to maintaining a good balance in parenting. Expressing our feelings (to an appropriate person, at an appropriate time) opens the door to figuring out solutions to day-to-day challenges.

When I was expecting my second baby, I recall another expectant mother showing up at my door doing a city-sponsored survey of families' needs. She and I discovered that our first-borns had almost the same birthday and that our new babies were due about the same time. We became friends almost overnight and remain so today, having traded childcare in those early days and shared many concerns and joys over the years. We joke that our now-grown children will have to take us to visit each other in our nursing homes just as we arranged their "play dates" when they were little.

In parenting, unlike writing, there are no first drafts, no scribbling down a few trial words of mothering or fathering then pressing the delete key. Everything counts. "No back-talk, no recall," as my sons would yell upon claiming the preferred seat in the car. How many times have I heard words coming out of my mouth and known they were wrong? Too many to count. What do I do differently today, as a parent? I remember to breathe and I ask more questions, of myself and of my sons. I also talk often with other parents and listen to their insights, especially the unwelcome ones. The ability to accept criticism is a valuable trait to develop, one I am still working on. I sure wish I didn't encounter so many "teachable moments!"

While we work to strike that difficult balance in our own households, what is going on in our neighbors' homes and in the homes of our children's classmates? Do relatives and friends support us in setting rules and holding our kids accountable for following them? If they don't, we can ask for this support. When they do, we can say thanks. Do our communities offer us formal and informal support in meeting the many challenges of raising a family? If they don't, we can advocate for this support. When they do, we can share the experience: tell friends and neighbors and mention successful programs to others who can spread the word.

In 1956 my father, Richard Odiorne, wrote a book, *Why They Came*, for the centennial celebration of my home town, Yellow Springs, Ohio. His opening and closing words capture the spirit of community that I believe we all want for ourselves and our children wherever we happen to live. It is the spirit that Parent Forum seeks to promote.

In the introduction, he stated the book's purpose as twofold: to present highlights of the town's history and

121

to affirm, for present and future residents, the town's "essential qualities of neighborliness, eagerness for new ideas, and simplicity of life in a busy world." In the closing paragraphs, he describes Yellow Springs as "a town in which quality of work can be more important than quantity; where people do not need to be caught in a race for bigness; where neighborliness promotes tolerance and understanding."

As our communities have become bigger, as our lives are too often invaded by news of violence if not directly by threat of violence or violence itself and as commercialism encroaches further into our communities and our lives, we can maintain a positive vision.

We can try to create loving and orderly homes. We can strive to be neighborly and tolerant. We can maintain an eagerness for new ideas. We can "live simply," as the expression goes, "so that others may simply live." I believe that we can and must do all of these things. I believe that Parents Forum is a strong partner with many others who, individually and collectively, care for children and support parents.

Resources

Resources

This list can serve as a starting point for you, your family or your parent group to find the support you need and the activities you want. We hope that these resources will also be useful to parenting educators. There is plenty of work for all of us! There are just under a hundred organizations listed, a somewhat random sampling with an North American bias due to our geographical location.

In this third edition, as in the second edition, program descriptions are replaced with websites and are as current as we are able to make them. If you put 'parents' in the search box on a site, you will usually find resources regarding parenting education, family support and programs for and about children. Among the new entries to the list are Association of Family and Conciliation Courts, Campaign for a Commercial-Free Childhood, Center for Children of Incarcerated Parents and National Military Family Association, all doing important work to support parents.

Government and nonprofit agencies at national, state or provincial and local levels provide a variety of services to families. Libraries, schools, after-school programs and community schools, museums, recreation centers and sports programs, as well as churches, temples and mosques may also offer programs for parents. Some larger employers have "work/life" programs and/or family resource centers that provide information and seminars on parenting. In many US cities and towns, there are parents' papers with event listings and informative articles.

Many agencies and parenting educators offer online newsletters and there are innumerable blogs, podcasts and social networks by and for parents. Check with your own trusted advisors, of course, before taking any free advice or purchasing goods or services. If I see a book on parenting that looks interesting, I often ask my local public library to purchase it, then not only can I read it, but others can also. One such book, *Raising Teens*, by Rae Simpson, deserves special mention and it is available in both English and Spanish online at web.mit.edu: enter 'raising teens' in the search box.

You may find helpful information through education associations (NAEYC and NAEVYC, National Associations for the Education of the Young Child and ...Very Young Child, for example), youth organizations (such as Boys & Girls Clubs, YMCA's, YWCA's and Family Y's, Girl Scouts / Boy Scouts, Big Brothers / Big Sisters), and seniors services.

Medical societies, notably the American Association of Pediatrics, have material and programs of interest to parents, as may unions, civic associations and cultural and immigrant community organizations. Volunteer centers are another excellent resource. Refugee and immigrant support centers in some areas may offer information and referral services for parents. You may also need problem-focused entities with parent support targeted to special needs and problems such as alcohol and other drug abuse (notably Al-Anon) and suicidality. If you have an urgent concern, you may find a parental stress line in your area offering immediate support and referrals by telephone. Call if you need to!

If you have corrections to any entries below or would like to recommend an addition to this list, please let us know. We welcome suggestions for an expanded resources listing that does justice to the many dedicated individuals offering parenting programs around the world.

Inclusion of a program in this list does not imply an endorsement of its approach or materials, nor does it imply that these programs endorse Parents Forum. The resources are offered with the implicit caveat: trust but verify.

If you do not find parenting programs in your area, why not seek out other like-minded individuals, find a host and sponsor and get one going!

We welcome your inquiries
at Parents Forum in Cambridge,
Massachusetts USA: www.parentsforum.org.

A

Alliance for a Healthier Generation
55 West 125th Street
New York NY 10027
www.healthiergeneration.org

Alliance for Childhood
P.O. Box 444
College Park MD 20741
www.allianceforchildhood.org

American Library Association
50 East Huron Street
Chicago IL 60611
www.ala.org

ASPIRA An Investment in Latino Youth
1444 I Street NW, Suite 800
Washington DC 20005 USA
www.aspira.org

Association of Family and
Conciliation Courts
6525 Grand Teton Plaza
Madison WI 53719
www.afccnet.org

At Home Dad
315 N. Belmont Avenue
Arlington Heights IL 60004
www.athomedad.org

B

Because I Love You / B.I.L.Y.
P.O. Box 2062
Winnetka CA 91396-2062
www.becauseiloveyou.org

Befrienders Worldwide
Upper Mill
Kingston Road
Ewell Surrey KT17 2AF United Kingdom
www.befrienders.org

C

Campaign for a Commercial-Free Childhood
53 Parker Hill Avenue
Boston MA 02120
www.commercialfreechildhood.org

Center for Children of Incarcerated Parents
P.O. Box 41-286
Eagle Rock CA 90041
www.e-ccip.org

Center for Civic Education
5143 Douglas Fir Road
Calabasas CA 91302-1440
www.civiced.org

Center for Screen-Time Awareness
1200 29th Street NW, Lower Level # 1
Washington DC 20007
www.screentime.org

Character Counts!
9841 Airport Boulevard, Suite 300
Los Angeles CA 90045
www.charactercounts.org

Child Welfare League of America
2345 Crystal Drive, Suite 250
Arlington VA 22202
www.cwla.org

Children's Defense Fund
25 E. Street NW
Washington DC 20001
www.childrensdefense.org

Children's Emotional Health Link
www.cehl.org

The Children's Partnership
1351 3rd Street Promenade, Suite 206
Santa Monica CA 90401
www.childrenspartnership.org

CIVICUS World Alliance for Citizen Participation
P.O. Box 933 Southdale
Johannesburg 2135 South Africa
www.civicus.org

Colombian Institute for Family Wellbeing
See Instituto Colombiano de Bienestar Familiar

Confederacion International de Apoyo Familiar / CIAF
See FAAF

D

The Drum Beat
This weekly electronic publication explores initiatives, ideas and trends in communication for development. See especially The Drum Beat issue #350 'Listening to Parents' an article by the author of this book and Jamesa Wagwau, columnist for Kampala New Vision, Uganda.
www.comminit.com

E

Everyday Democracy
111 Founders Plaza, Suite 1403
East Hartford CT 06108
www.everyday-democracy.org

F

FAAF/CIAF International Confederation for Family Support
Calle 33 No.1978 La Plata
PCIA Buenos Aires Argentina
www.esperanza.org.ar

Families and Work Institute
267 Fifth Avenue, Floor 2
New York NY 10016
www.familiesandwork.org

Families First
99 Bishop Allen Drive
Cambridge MA 02139
www.families-first.org

FAMILIS World Organization for Families
4837 rue Boyer, Suite 110
Montreal PQ Canada H2J 3E6
www.familis.org

Fathers and Families Coalition of America
39 East Jackson
Phoenix AZ 85004
www.azffc.org

Federation Internationale pour l'Education des Parents / FIEP
See International Federation

The Foundation for Grandparenting
108 Farnham Road
Ojai CA 93023
www.grandparenting.org

Fourth World, International Movement ATD
114 avenue du Général Leclerc
F-95480 Pierrelaye France
www.atd-fourthworld.org

G

Global Nomads Group
381 Broadway, 4th Floor
New York NY 10013
www.gng.org

The Go-To Mom
P.O. Box 40494
Pasadena CA 91114
www.thegotomom.tv

The Good Men Project
143 Newbury Street, 6th Floor
Boston MA 02116
www.goodmenproject.org

Grandparent Information Center, AARP
601 E Street NW
Washington DC 20049
www.aarp.org

H

Hand-in-Hand Parenting
P.O. Box 1279
Palo Alto CA 94302
www.handinhandparenting.org

Resources

The Hardiness Institute
4199 Campus Drive, Suite 550
Irvine CA 92612
www.hardinessinstitute.com

Harvard Family Research Project
3 Garden Street
Cambridge MA 02138
www.hfrp.org

Hostelling International
www.hihostels.com -and- www.hiusa.org

I

Instituto Colombiano de Bienestar Familiar
Avenida carrera 68, No.64 C-75
87 Bogotá Colombia
www.icbf.gov.co

Interaction International
P. O. Box 863
Wheaton IL 60189
www.interactionintl.org

International Association for Volunteer Effort
Fl.1, No.31, Sec.1
Zhong-xiao East Road
Taipei Taiwan (ROC)
www.iave.org

International Commission on Couple and Family Relations
1 Blythe Mews
Blythe Road
London W14 0NW United Kingdom
www.iccfr.org

International Federation for Parent Education
1 Avenue Leon Journault
F-92318 Sevres Cedex France
www.fiep-ifpe.fr

J

Janera, curating global conversations
www.janera.com

Join Together
580 Harrison Avenue, 3rd Floor
Boston MA 02118
www.jointogether.org

Jump$tart Coalition for Personal Financial Literacy
919 18th Street NW, Suite 300
Washington DC 20006
www.jumpstart.org

K

Kiwanis International
3636 Woodview Trace
Indianapolis IN 46268-3196
www.kiwanis.org

Resources

L

La Leche League
P.O. Box 4079
Schaumburg IL 60168-4079
www.llli.org

Lions Clubs International
300 22nd Street
Oak Brook IL 60523-8842
www.lionsclubs.org

N

National Center for Family Literacy
325 West Main Street, Suite 3000
Louisville KY 40202-4237
www.famlit.org

National Center for Fathering
P.O. Box 413888
Kansas City MO 64141
www.fathers.com

National Council on Family Relations
3989 Central Avenue NE
Minneapolis MN 55421
www.ncfr.org

National Effective Parenting Initiative
Center for Improvement in Child Caring
11331 Ventura Boulevard, Suite 103
Studio City CA 91604-3147
www.effectiveparentingusa.org

National Family Caregivers Association
10400 Connecticut Avenue, Suite 500
Kensington MD 20895-3944
www.nfcacares.org

National Fatherhood Initiative
101 Lake Forest Boulevard, Suite 360
Gaithersburg MD 20877
www.fatherhood.org

National Foster Parent Association
2313 Tacoma Avenue S.
Tacoma WA 98402
www.nfpainc.org

National Institute on Media and the Family
606 24th Avenue South, Suite 606
Minneapolis MN 55454
www.mediafamily.org

National Military Family Association
2500 North Van Dorn Street, Suite 102
Alexandria VA 22302-1601
www.nmfa.org

National Parent Teacher Association
541 N Fairbanks Court, Suite 1300
Chicago IL 60611-3396
www.pta.org

National Parenting Education Network
c/o ECAP / Children's Research Center
51 Gerty Drive
Champaign IL 61820-7469
www.npen.org

NGO Committee on Mental Health
www.mentalhealthngo.org

Resources

P

The Parenting Journey
c/o The Family Center
366 Somerville Avenue
Somerville MA 02143
www.thefamilycenterinc.org

Parenting Publications of America
1970 E. Grand Avenue, Suite 330
El Segundo CA 90245
www.parentingpublications.org

Parenting UK
Unit 431 Highgate Studios
53-79 Highgate Road
London NW5 1TL United Kingdom
www.parentinguk.org

Parents Action for Children
P.O. Box 2096
Culver City CA 90231
www.parentsaction.org

Parents Anonymous
675 W. Foothill Boulevard, Suite 220
Claremont CA 91711-3475
www.parentsanonymous.org

Parents, Families and
Friends of Lesbians and Gays
1726 M Street NW, Suite 400
Washington DC 20036
www.pflag.org

Parents Forum
144 Pemberton Street
Cambridge MA 02140
www.parentsforum.org

Parents Helping Parents
108 Water Street
Watertown MA 02472
www.parentshelpingparents.org

The Parents Journal
a national radio series
www.parentsjournal.com

Parents Television Council
707 Wilshire Boulevard #2075
Los Angeles CA 90017
www.parentstv.org

Parents Toolshop
P.O. Box 343
Springboro OH 45066
www.parentstoolshop.com

Parents Without Partners
1650 South Dixie Highway, Suite 402
Boca Raton FL 33432
www.parentswithoutpartners.org

**Partnership for
America's Economic Success**
c/o The Pew Charitable Trusts
901 E Street NW, 10th Floor
Washington DC 20004
www.partnershipforsuccess.org

Playing for Keeps
c/o Association of Children's Museums
1300 L Street NW, Suite 975
Washington DC 20005
www.childrensmuseums.org

Prepare Tomorrow's Parents
454 NE Third Street
Boca Raton FL 33432
www.preparetomorrowsparents.org

R

Respect for Parents Day
P.O. Box 1563
Lancaster CA 93539
members.tripod.com/MarilynDalrymple/index-4.html

Room to Read
111 Sutter Street, 16th Floor
San Francisco CA 94104
www.roomtoread.org

Rotary International
1560 Sherman Avenue
Evanston IL 60201
www.rotary.org

S

Samaritans USA
P.O. Box 1259 Madison Square Station
New York NY 10159
www.ncsp.org
See also Befrienders Worldwide and SPAN

Samaritans of Boston
/Samariteens
141 Tremont Street, 7th Floor
Boston MA 02111
www.samaritansofboston.org

Search Institute
615 First Avenue NE
Minneapolis MN 55413
www.search-institute.org

Service and Research Institute on
Family and Children / SERFAC
1/157, Manimangalam Road
Varadharajapuram
Chennai 600 048 India

Société de recherche en
orientation humaine
2120 Sherbrooke est
Montreal PQ Canada
www.sroh.org

Suicide Prevention Awareness
Network / SPAN
1010 Vermont Avenue NW, Suite 408
Washington DC 20005
www.spanusa.org

T

Task Force for Global Health
325 Swanton Way
Decatur GA 30030
www.taskforce.org

Resources

Toughlove International
www.toughlove.com

Tufts University
Child & Family Web Guide
105 College Avenue
Medford MA 02155
www.cfw.tufts.edu

U

UNESCO: UN Educational Scientific
and Cultural Organization
Under 'education' look for publications on early
childhood, family policy and other topics
www.unesco.org

United Nations Programme on the Family
Two United Nations Plaza, Room DC2-1302
New York NY 10017
www.un.org/esa/socdev/family

U.S. Department of Education
www.ed.gov/pubs

V

Vegetarian Society
Parkdale, Dunham Road
Altrincham
Cheshire WA14 4QG United Kingdom
www.vegsoc.org

Vienna NGO Committee on the Family
Josefstrasse 13
A-3100 St. Poelten Austria
www.viennafamilycommittee.org

Viva Rio
Rua do Russel, 76 - Glória
CEP: 222210-010
Rio de Janeiro RJ, Brazil
www.vivario.org.br

Wheelock College
200 The Riverway
Boston MA 02215
www.wheelock.edu

World Learning
P.O. Box 676, 1 Kipling Road
Brattleboro VT 05302
www.worldlearning.org

Young Audiences
115 East 92nd Street
New York NY 10128-1688
www.youngaudiences.org

Z

Zero to Three
National Center for Infants, Toddlers and Families
2000 M Street NW, Suite 200
Washington DC 20036
www.zerotothree.org

Index

Index

Index

Index

Index

positive experiences, remembering, 77
Prepare Tomorrow's Parents, **138**
prizes, as tool for community building, 30

Q

questions, asking
   balancing inquiry and advocacy, 71–72
   being specific, 55
   tone of voice, 73–74
questions, in Parents Forum agenda
   what are your household rules?, 79–83
   what are your household values?, 77–79
   what changes have you experienced lately, what changes do you expect?, 86–88
   what concerns or troubles you about your family, 62–63
   what do you like about your family?, 60–62
   what happens when someone joins or leaves your family?, 83–86

R

Raising Teens (Simpson), 125
relationships, balancing need for, 6, 34–37.
   See also support
resources
   alphabetical listing of, 126–141
   education associations, 125
   experts, professionals, 124–125
   government and nonprofit agencies, 124
   medical societies, 125
   sharing information about, 106
Respect for Parents Day, **138**
Reviving Ophelia (Pipher), 28
roleplay, 30, 64–65, 113–114
Room to Read, **138**
Rotary International, **138**
Roxbury, Mass., 32

as Parents Forum theme, 24
parents' needs for, 3, 16–17

T

Task Force for Global Health, **139**
teenagers, parenting needs, 74–75
Telling Our Own Stories workshops, 112–113
ten, counting to, 43
thankfulness. See appreciation, cultivating
therapeutic communities, 10–12, 22–23
thoughts vs. feelings, 46
time, parents' need for, 3
"time outs," 95
tone of voice. *See also* language, word choices
    when asking questions, 73–74
    when responding to events, 16, 72
    yelling, 82
Toughlove® International, **140**
toy "vacations," 65
transitions, passages, learning to handle, 83–86
Tufts University Child & Family Web Guide, **140**
24-hour rule, 64

U

UNESCO, **140**
United Nations Programme on the Family, **140**
United Nations, International Year of the
    Family, 104–105, 116
U.S. Department of Education, **140**

V

values, household
    identifying and naming, 77–79
    values and rules statements, 82
    writing down and posting, 96

Acknowledgements
and Afterword

Acknowledgements

My gratitude list starts with my parents, Dick and Louise Odiorne, no longer living, whom I thank for their energy and inspiration. I am happy to have known all four of my grandparents, Kitty Grandmother and Grandfather George Harris, Grandfather Ralph and Grandmother Helen Odiorne. I cherish a childhood shared with my sister Corinne and my brother Ken. Four people who helped me along the way, Beverly and Read Viemeister, Florence O'Hare and Herman Feshbach deserve special mention. I learned a great deal from each of them... how to be as well as what to do, in life.

Joe, my ex-husband, gave me the chance to be a mother, and I am grateful to him every day for Rich, Luke and Michael. Joe also suggested that one of his Ethiopian students take a room in my house and Merid Seifu became a wonderful brother to our three. Thanks so much to the four of you for your patience and love in raising me as a parent.

So many people have been helpful to me personally and to our organization, since 1992 when Parents Forum was founded, that the list is very long, too long in fact to print here. It will appear on our website, however. One friend whose name must be mentioned is Christine Bates, the program co-founder: without her help and advice Parents Forum would not have been created or lasted this long.

Anxieties that too often made me feel like a beggar fade away in the warmth of the encouragement that many people have shown for this work over many years. If wishes were horses, beggars would ride. Here I am, not riding, but writing! Even better.

160

In the nine years since we first printed this book much has changed in publishing and we decided to publish this edition by print on demand. Minor changes here include using Microsoft clip art (with permission, of course) for the animals that depict the 'stages of learning, stages of life' in our workshop curriculum. We have kept the look of the first edition which benefited from Martha Mulligan Hooper's editing, Marie Sheridan's and Martina Marek's illustrations, Fletcher Moore's typesetting and his choice of Bookman Old Style typeface. Top-quality design and file preparation by Jana Bull for the first, second and third editions have made them happen. Thanks to you all.

Parents Forum program materials and services are protected by registered trademarks and are available for use through licensing agreements. We welcome inquiries from parents and others interested in organizing Parents Forum programs in their own communities. We especially welcome inquiries regarding translating our materials into languages other than English.

This book may be printed and distributed at no charge under a Creative Commons license.
See details on the Disclaimer, Licenses and Support page.

Contact us:

Parents Forum
144 Pemberton Street
Cambridge MA 02140 USA

info@parentsforum.org
www.parentsforum.org

CPSIA information can be obtained at www.ICGtesting.com

263827BV00004B/6/P